D0065029

Basic Nature

Basic Nature

Andrew Scott

Basil Blackwell

Copyright © Andrew Scott, 1991

First published 1991

Basil Blackwell Ltd
108 Cowley Road, Oxford, OX4 1JF, UK

Basil Blackwell, Inc.
3 Cambridge Center
Cambridge, Massachusetts 02142, USA

British Library Cataloguing in Publication Data

A CIP catalogue record for this book is available from the British Library.

Library of Congress Cataloging in Publication Data

Scott, Andrew, 1955–
Basic nature / Andrew Scott.
   p.   cm.
Includes bibliographical references and index.
ISBN 0–631–17362–5
1. Science – Popular works.   2. Physics – Popular works.   I. Title.
Q126.S38   1991   90–49424
500–dc20   CIP

Typeset in 10 on 12 pt Palatino
by Hope Services (Abingdon) Ltd,
Printed in Great Britain by
T. J. Press (Padstow) Ltd, Padstow, Cornwall

Contents

Preface

This is a minimalist's survey of the foundations of science. It is intended to convey the essence of the scientific view of Nature in as few pages as possible.

Perhaps the most common fate of a popular science book is to be bought in a burst of enthusiasm and then disappointedly discarded as soon as difficult ideas and concepts arise without proper explanation. This book aims to explain these most fundamental concepts of science, providing a useful overview of science in itself, but also preparing its readers for any deeper investigation they may wish, or perhaps be required, to undertake. For readers who already possess a fair grasp of the subjects covered, the book should provide useful summaries of, and perhaps fresh insights into, things they already know a bit about.

My hope is that the book will be particularly useful to the non-scientist interested in science, and also to students at school and university.

This is not the place to look to for a history of science, nor for any deep insight into the process of science, the philosophy of science or the minds and methods of the scientists whose results are reported. It is the place to look to for a brief distillation of the essential foundations of theory and discovery which underpin our understanding of Nature.

I would encourage readers to read the book from the beginning to the end, rather than jumping around the chapters erratically. I would also encourage them to push all pre-existing knowledge and conceptions of science to the back of their minds for a while. They should let the book give a fresh view as it steadily reveals the foundations of science.

Andrew Scott

Acknowledgements

I would like to thank everyone at Basil Blackwell involved in the planning and production of the book, especially Mark Allin and Sue Martin.

Thanks also to Margaret, for her continuing help and support.

1 Spacetime

There is something funny about space and there is something funny about time. Albert Einstein will tell you about it if you read his 'popular exposition' *Relativity*, first published in 1916, whose pages can put the voice of the dead genius into your mind, across the barrier of space and time. We can explore the essence, however, in just this short chapter, which describes the strangeness Einstein discovered in the structure of space and time, and how it led to the union of these two seemingly distinct phenomena into the hybrid we now refer to as spacetime.

We must accept at the outset that our very restricted experience of space and time deceives us into beliefs about them which are false, no matter how obvious and true they may seem to be. The main deceiver is the ponderous sluggishness of the events we can see and experience directly, compared to the speed at which some things happen. We are normally limited to experiencing space and time through the behaviour of objects which move very slowly, relative to one another, compared with the speeds they could attain. We glean all our everyday experience of the symphony of the universe from its slow movements, and this profoundly misleads us about the real music of the spheres.

If we jump into a car and drive along the road at 50 miles per hour, we may be overtaken by another car. Suppose we were able to measure how fast this car was overtaking us and then moving away from us. If the answer was 30 miles per hour, we might reasonably expect that its speed relative to the ground would be 50 + 30, i.e. 80 miles per hour, but it would not. It would be very close to that, so close we could never hope to detect any discrepancy, but the true speed relative to the ground would be slightly different from the speed we expected by naively adding the overtaker's speed relative to us to our speed relative to the ground. Speeds, or more correctly 'velocities' (meaning speeds in any given direction), do not in reality add together as neatly as that, but we are deceived into thinking that they do because at such slow speeds the discrepancies are very small. If our cars were able to move much faster, at speeds approaching the speed of light, the discrepancy would be much more obvious and we would gain a better intuitive grasp of the real nature of space, time and spacetime as we drove around in our cars or travelled in trains and planes. As objects begin to move relative to one another at speeds that are a significant fraction of the speed of light, things happen that defy our common sense.

How can we learn about and try to understand these strange things that happen when we move at speeds close to the speed of light? The first step is to realize that in fact all of us really *are* moving at the speed of light relative to something we experience all the time – we are moving at the speed of light relative to the light that rushes past us! So we can use light as an 'object' which moves at the speed of light, and 'past which' we move at the speed of light, to test our assumptions about space and time and speeds.

Suppose we are back in our car, travelling along at 50 miles per hour, busy measuring the speed at which various things are overtaking us. A car overtakes us going 30 miles per hour faster than us, so we expect its speed relative to the ground to be 50 + 30, i.e. 80 miles per hour. Then a jet plane sweeps past and away from us at 600 miles per hour, so we expect its speed relative to the ground to be 650 miles per hour. Our imaginary perfect measuring apparatus is even sophisticated enough to measure the speed of a satellite streaking overhead at 20,000 miles per hour relative to us, and so, we presume, at 20,050 miles per hour relative to the ground. Finally, we measure the speed at which light from the sunset behind us is overtaking us, and we find it to be rushing past at around 670 million miles per hour. Whatever the precise value was, we would obviously expect that anyone standing at the roadside would find the speed of light moving in our direction to be 50 miles per hour faster than the speed at which it moves past us; yet they do not. A roadside observer would find the light to be moving at *exactly* the same speed past them as we find it to be moving past us! How can we both come up with exactly the same figure, when we in our car are surely moving along *with* the light at 50 miles per hour? What happened to the difference of 50 miles per hour? Where did it go?

Before dealing with that puzzle, I should emphasize the phenomenon that gave rise to it – the constancy of the speed of light regardless of who measures it and regardless of how they are moving. This is a real and well-verified phenomenon, not some tentative hypothesis, and it is the phenomenon which led Albert Einstein to invent his theory of 'relativity', for the predictions of that theory to be experimentally confirmed, and so for our view of space and time to be radically altered. Two sets of apparatus able to measure the speed of light will always record exactly the same speed, even if, for example, they are examining the light from the sun while positioned opposite each other on the earth's equator so that, due to the earth's rotation, one is travelling very quickly towards the sun and the other is moving equally quickly away from it (see figure 1.1). This clearly defies our common-sense expectations, which tell us that the speed of light recorded by the first set of apparatus should be significantly greater than the speed recorded by the other. In all other measurements the results are the same. The speed of light is always found to be the same regardless of how the apparatus measuring it is moving. It is true that the speed does change a little depending on what *medium* the light is moving through – it moves slightly faster through the near vacuum of space, for example, than it does through air. Despite this, the essential baffling point remains that the speed of light through any given medium is always measured to be the same by two sets of apparatus moving relative to one another.

This puzzle of the constancy of the speed of light was not discovered by Albert Einstein. The great Scottish physicist James Clerk Maxwell had predicted in the 1860s that light must move through space as a wave-like disturbance at a certain fixed velocity, and he reached this conclusion simply on the basis of theoretical calculations. In 1887 the theoretical conclusion was confirmed by an experiment performed by the German/American physicist Albert Michelson and the American chemist Edward Morley. This celebrated 'Michelson-Morley' experiment looked for evidence of light waves travelling at different speeds in different directions due to the effects of the earth's motion, in essence much as described above, although the experimental details were a bit more subtle. Michelson and Morley found no evidence of any speed difference, however, thus confirming the constancy of the speed of light regardless of how the source of the light or observers of the light are moving.

Although Einstein did not discover the constancy of the speed of light, he did think deeply about the puzzle this result presented, and he thought about it in a very different way from most other people. The essential mystery is, what happens to the difference in the speed of light expected when observers such as ourselves in our car and our colleague by the roadside both measure the speed of light from the setting sun? How can two observers measure the speed of light to be the

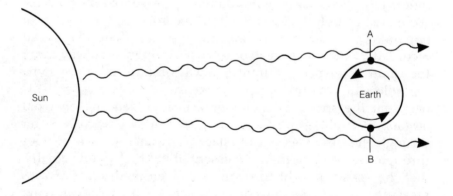

Figure 1.1 The speed of light through any medium is always found to be the same by different observers regardless of how they are moving. Observers at A and B on the equator of the rotating earth will measure the same speed for the light arriving from the sun.

same, despite the fact that they are moving relative to one another? One natural reaction to it is to say 'there is clearly something funny about light.' Another view might suggest that the result must be wrong, due to some subtle mistake or illusion. Einstein accepted the result at face value, began with the assumption that the speed of light really must be the same for all observers, regardless of their motion, and investigated where that assumption would lead. By assuming that there was nothing 'funny about light' he discovered that there was something decidedly funny about the space the light travels through, and the time it takes to do so – funny, that is, compared to what we expect on the basis of everyday experience.

The heart of the dilemma is the speed of light, and all speeds are defined as the *distance* that something moves in a given *time*. The way out of our difficulties is to realize that two people moving relative to one another could measure the same value for the speed of light if the distances (i.e. the amount of space) and the times they measure are somehow altered. Putting our faith in the constancy of the speed of light means that we must lose faith in our everyday notions of space and time.

The 'funny' thing about space and time turned out to be this: distances appear to become increasingly shorter, when measured in the direction of motion, as things begin to move relative to us; while time appears to flow more slowly for things moving relative to us. In other words, as objects begin to move relative to us they appear to us to experience a contraction of space and a dilation of time.

That deserves more consideration. Suppose we are on a spaceship and we can carefully examine, using some sort of remote sensing apparatus, events on another spaceship moving past us at some significant fraction of the speed of light. Our equipment would tell us that the spaceship was significantly shorter than it had been when we had measured it earlier when we were both stationary on the ground; and it would also tell us that the spaceship's clock was running slow, as indeed would be all of the events on the spaceship, such as the rate of chemical reactions and thus the ageing processes within anyone on board. 'Ahah!', we might say, so that is why they measure the speed of light to be the same as we do, their distances and clocks have altered in such a way as to make the results agree! Their space and their time appear to be different from ours! Their space has contracted in the direction of their motion, and their time has dilated to make their clocks run slow; in fact, they appear to have lost some space and gained some time!

This might cause us great puzzlement, but at least it might make us think it could resolve our original dilemma, the dilemma of how we can both come up with the same value for the speed of light. We might argue that this happens because they are using distances and clocks that are different from ours. We may even be tempted to say that they are using distances and clocks that are somehow 'wrong'; yet there is a trap leading to further perplexity awaiting us. As far as anyone on board the other spaceship is concerned, it is us who are moving, while they feel themselves to be stationary. So as they examined our distances and our clocks, they would measure *our* distances as being shortened in the direction of our apparent motion, and they would see *our* clocks to be running slow. One of the major tenets of Einstein's theory (although Einstein was certainly not the first to suggest it) is that all motion is relative, so that no one can regard themselves as truly stationary and anything else as actually moving. If someone is moving relative to us, then we are moving to an equal extent relative to them, and no one person is in the privileged position of being able to say that they are really stationary. So whatever strange things we see happening to people moving relative to us must be identical to the strange things they see happening to us, always assuming that our motions are constant and that we are neither speeding up nor slowing down nor changing direction.

At this stage one is tempted to shake one's head and think such things as, 'If I see someone's distances shrinking and clocks slowing down, they should see my distances grow larger and my clocks speeding up. How on earth can they see the same as I do? It doesn't make sense!' Unfortunately, if it doesn't make sense to us that is because we do not have the sense to understand it, because however hard we shake our heads it remains true – these effects have been well confirmed by experiment.

We can be nudged towards acceptance by considering a different, though in some ways similar, effect that we have all experienced so often that we can accept it as everyday common sense. If I am standing a mile away from you, I appear very small to you compared to the six foot four that I consider myself to be; and yet to me, *you* would appear diminished in size by just the same extent as I appear diminished to you. Anyone unused to the effects of perspective in three dimensions might be as baffled by that effect as we can be by the ones discussed above, at least until they had experienced it themselves and thought about it until it became utterly self-evident and reasonable. An alternative analogy, much closer to the true situation and so hopefully even more persuasive, will be considered shortly.

To summarize, by keeping faith in the genuine constancy of the speed of light, Einstein discovered something remarkable about space and time: things that are moving relative to us appear to have undergone a contraction of distance in the direction of their motion, and a dilation of time, such that we measure their distances to be shorter than ours and find their clocks running slower than ours.

If we return to the original puzzle of our measurements of the speed of things overtaking our car as we ourselves travelled at 50 miles per hour relative to the ground, we should now appreciate that we were mistaken in assuming that we could naively add speeds in the way that led to our puzzlement. If we are travelling along at 50 miles per hour and are overtaken by something going away from us at 30 miles per hour, it is *not* moving at 80 miles per hour relative to the ground, but at fractionally, imperceptibly, less than that because, as viewed from the ground, our measuring apparatus uses slightly contracted distances and a slightly slower clock and so our measurements are 'wrong', as far as anyone standing by the roadside is concerned. This effect increases as the speed of the things overtaking us increases until, when both ourselves and our roadside colleague examine an overtaking beam of light, the effect is sufficient to completely cancel out our 50 miles per hour speed relative to the ground – both observers find the speed of light to be the same. So where has the 50 miles per hour gone, as we wondered earlier? It has been eaten up by the contraction of space and dilation of time that observers observe in anything moving relative to themselves.

Einstein's discovery that we see space contracted and time dilated for moving objects was not the end of his theoretical adventure, but just the beginning, for it led on to further momentous revelations uncovered both by himself and by other people who developed his discoveries further. Some are discussed in other chapters, but there is one which must be considered here: the revelation that space and time cannot be regarded as two distinct phenomena, but as an intriguing unity which is known as spacetime.

To investigate the link that unites space and time into spacetime, we should first reflect on our notions of space and time individually. Einstein cut boldly through a semantic morass by defining space and time with straightforward simplicity: 'space is what we measure with a measuring rod and time is what we measure with a clock.' Such clarity renders redundant endless philosophical debate about the two phenomena, but we should give the meanings of space and time a little more thought.

Physicists make a clear distinction between space and nothing at all. Space, to them, is not nothingness. It is a phenomenon distinct from nothingness, in other words distinct from the complete absence of any phenomenon at all. A physicist can describe space with equations which show how it can grow, or shrink, or change its characteristics in other subtle ways. So we must think of the 'vacuum' of space as something, not the nothing which it is normally assumed to be.

Apart from that distinction, our everyday notion of what is meant by space is perfectly adequate to understand what follows. We are all familiar with the idea that we occupy a space of three 'dimensions', which simply means that we have the opportunity to move up and down, forward and backwards, or from side to side. More technical language would say that these are the three 'degrees of freedom' available to our movement. Technical discussions also point out that we can describe the movement of anything in space, relative to its original position or some other standard reference point, by using just three numbers to quantify how far the movement has taken the object up or down, forwards or back, or sideways – each of the three numbers corresponding to motion in just one dimension of space.

At first sight, time seems to be a quite distinct phenomenon from space. It is certainly a *different* phenomenon from space, but the two are more closely related than we might expect. Time is our measure of the rate of change. We take some standard and repetitive change, such as the rotation of the arms of a clock, or the vibration of a crystal, and then we measure the 'time' taken for all other changes by relating it to an amount of change in our clock, or our crystal, or whatever. Since measurements of time can be represented by a single number, indicating the time elapsed from one event to another, it is easy to label it as another single 'dimension', and to appreciate that the time and place of an event can be pinned down by quoting four numbers corresponding to its location in the three dimensions of space and the one dimension of time. So the movement of anything in space and time can be specified by four numbers referring to movement in these four dimensions from some starting point, just as the movement of anything in space could be specified by giving three numbers describing movement through the three dimensions of space.

There is much more to the relationship between space and time, however, than the simple idea that there are three dimensions of one and one of the other which together pin down any event in both space and time. In fact, we have already seen evidence of a much closer relationship, although its full implications may not yet have occurred to you. We have seen that in anything moving relative to us, some space appears to grow smaller ('contract') while time appears to grow longer ('dilate'). What we are actually seeing is space *becoming* time, demonstrating a unity and interchangeability between the two which was unsuspected before Einstein prepared people to appreciate it. Einstein himself didn't appreciate it fully until it was properly established by the Russian/German mathematician Hermann Minkowski. Minkowski was actually one of Einstein's teachers while Einstein was a student at the Zurich polytechnic, and after the student had taught the teacher something, namely the theory of relativity, the teacher came back and pointed out how the work could have been finished off better! Minkowski developed a system of geometry which set the unity and interchangeability of space and time into a proper mathematical framework. This unity and interchangeability needs further exploration and explanation.

Return for a moment to the simple world of three-dimensional space, and suppose that you are looking at a model spaceship held before you in your hand. You are looking at it side on, seeing that it is quite long and thin with its sharp nose to your left and its tail fins to your right. Now you rotate it a little to get a better view of the tail, and as you rotate it its length, or in other words its extension in the sideways dimension, appears to diminish. Try this with a pencil if it is unclear (or a model spaceship if you have one to hand!). Now you know, or you think you know, that the model is not 'really' getting any shorter as you rotate it. All that is happening is that *its length is being rotated into another dimension*, the forwards and backwards dimension relative to you. To you, however, the spaceship is contracting in the sideways dimension and dilating (growing larger) in the forwards and backwards dimension. This effect is a very familiar one to anyone living in a three-dimensional world – something which appears long and thin from the side can appear very short and stubby from the front and back, because as it is rotated, or as we walk round it, its original length moves into another dimension as viewed from our standpoint.

We have a very persuasive analogy here for what happens when things begin to move relative to us, except instead of some contraction of length in one dimension of space causing a dilation of length in another dimension of space, the contraction of length causes a dilation in the 'fourth' dimension of time. So the three dimensions of space and one dimension of time really are much more intimately related or connected than we might think. It seems that it is possible for some distance in space to 'rotate away' into some length of time. Just as the length of a spaceship can be rotated away from us into another dimension of the three-dimensional world of space, so some of the length of a moving spaceship can be rotated away from us into time in the four-dimensional world which we must call spacetime.

So we begin to realize why we are forced to consider space and time to be somehow united into the mysterious four-dimensional world of spacetime. It is mysterious and mystifying to us only because we do not experience the effects of its existence in our sluggish everyday world. If we were very flat creatures living on a flat landscape and unable to look up or down, we might be completely baffled if someone lifted us up so that the effects of rotation into the third dimension above us were suddenly revealed. Similarly we can be baffled when first introduced to the effects of rotation of some space into the fourth dimension of time – baffled as we suddenly see moving clocks run slow as they contract in their direction of motion. Such rotations happen all the time, however, only to such a tiny extent that we never notice them (although the 'rotations' involved are a bit more geometrically subtle than the rotations in three dimensions that we are used to). As you drive along in your car you are rotated in spacetime relative to the people standing in the street. To them, a little of the length of your car has been lost from view, only to reappear as a slight lengthening of the time your watch takes to tick out each second; although only if your car were able to reach a significant fraction of the speed of light would the effect become noticeable.

We live in a world of space and time, a world of spacetime, whose unity as a four-dimensional arena is real and rigorously testable, although it is certainly not obvious to us. We cannot visualize it because we have no direct experience of it, so we should not be too hard on ourselves if we find it a little difficult to comprehend. But we should not make the mistake of dismissing phenomena simply because we find it hard to visualize how they can exist. Spacetime, not mere space, is the true arena into which we are born, and in which we live out our lives.

2 Mass

What is there to our universe, other than the space and time – the spacetime – which serves as the arena in which things can happen? The obvious answer is that there are objects: there are so called 'physical' things such as stars and planets and plants and people and rocks and stones, all composed of the stuff we call 'matter'. There are other more subtle things present as well, such as light, but the most obvious occupants of the spacetime arena are the material objects made of matter; but what do we mean by 'matter'?

A dictionary of science might tell us that matter is the name given to anything that has the property of 'mass' and also some extension in space and time. The last point indicates that matter must have some volume and must survive for a certain amount of time, but what is this phenomenon called mass? We return to our dictionary for help and discover that mass is the name given to a measure of how much effort is needed to change the motion of an object, or in other words to make it accelerate or decelerate. Technically, the mass of an object is a measure of how much 'force' is needed to change its motion by a given amount, so it is a measure of an object's resistance to motion. For 'how much force' you can loosely read 'how much of a push', although the concept of force is discussed more fully in chapter 3.

So things which need a push (or pull) by some force in order to change their motion are said to possess mass, with the mass (measured in kilograms) being proportional to the force required to bring about a certain amount of change in the motion. We are all familiar with many things that require a push or pull in order to change their motion, in fact it is hard to think of anything that does not; but why should this be? This puzzle, and it really is a puzzle, is known as the puzzle of the origin of inertia, for inertia is the name given to the tendency of objects with mass to neither accelerate nor decelerate unless some force is applied to them. Of course moving things do slow down in the everyday world, but only because of the forces of friction that make them do so. In a frictionless world our cars could coast in neutral along a level road for ever.

Inertia, however, is just one aspect of the phenomenon we call mass. The other aspect involves the familiar force of gravity, through which any two objects are attracted towards one another. A full dictionary definition of mass will tell us that not only is it a measure of how much force is needed to change the motion of an object, but it is also a measure of what contribution an object makes to the gravitational force of attraction between itself and any other object. The mass of an object determines how strong will be the gravity associated with it. Resistance to change in motion and the creation of gravity are the two phenomena associated with mass.

This presents us with a second puzzle: why and how do objects with mass give rise to the attractive force of gravity that surrounds them? But the puzzles do not end there. Exploration of dictionary definitions of mass will soon lead us to sub-entries entitled 'rest mass' and 'relativistic mass'. What are these two types of mass? The dictionary may tell us that rest mass is the mass of objects at rest, which seems sensible enough, but that relativistic mass is the total mass of a *moving* object, a mass that is larger than the object's rest mass. What bizarre phenomenon is this? How can objects put on mass just because they are moving?

We must explore all these puzzles, although the one concerning gravity is left to its own chapter (chapter 4). Before commencing the exploration, however, the distinction between mass and the more everyday related concept of weight should be pointed out. In science mass is not the same thing as weight, although there are circumstances in which they appear to be the same. We weigh something by placing it on a set of scales and measuring how forcefully it is pulled towards the earth by the earth's gravity. That is what weight is, a measure of the *force* with which an object is pulled downwards. That force depends entirely on the mass of the object – the more mass an object has the greater its weight will be – but the two concepts are different. To grasp the difference, imagine we transport the object and scales to the moon, where gravity is much weaker. The weight of the object will be less than on earth, but its mass will be unchanged. Mass is a fundamental measure of the tendency of an object to resist change in its motion and generate its own gravity. Weight is a more fickle quantity that varies from place to place, depending on the gravitational force prevailing at each location. Mass and weight are easily confused because they can be quoted in the same units. On earth the weight of a 1-kilogram mass is referred to as 1 kilogram, but on the moon the same 1-kilogram mass would register a considerably smaller weight.

Back to our puzzles, and firstly to the distinction between an object's rest mass and relativistic mass. What is the origin of the difference between an object's mass at rest and its mass when in motion? We are looking here at one of the further revelations of Albert Einstein. In developing his theories about space and time as discussed in chapter 1, Einstein discovered that not only is there something funny about space and time, but there is also something funny about mass. 'Funny', that is, compared to our everyday expectations.

One fundamental revelation of Einstein's theorizing was that the speed of light is not only the same for everyone, but is the maximum speed that anything can ever attain. The speed of light presents a natural and seemingly unbreakable speed limit which everything in the universe must obey. This threw up an interesting conflict with the 'classical' physics of the day, concerning the phenomenon known as momentum. If the mass (in kilograms) of a moving object is multiplied by the value of its velocity (in metres per second) the resulting quantity is known as the object's momentum. If the moving object is then subjected to a further push, or in other words another force, in the direction of its movement, then classical physics tells us that its momentum must increase in direct proportion to the force. In the everyday world this increase in momentum can clearly be attributed to the increase in velocity of the object brought about by the push. But suppose we give the object repeated pushes until it begins to approach the speed of light. Since the speed of light is the barrier through which the object's speed can never pass, successive pushes must result in steadily lessening accelerations, so that no matter how many pushes are given the object can never break through the speed of light barrier. So we have a dilemma: how can the momentum increase by the same amount with each push, if the resulting increase in speed, and therefore velocity, is constantly decreasing? Since the momentum is the mass multiplied by the velocity, one possible solution is to suggest that as things go faster their mass must increase. This would allow the increase in the mass to compensate for the fact that the velocity is increasing by less with each push. Strange though it may seem, this is the true answer, for it has been well confirmed in experiments using fast-moving sub-atomic particles. Objects really do get more massive, and therefore heavier, as they move more quickly. At everyday low speeds the effect is unnoticable, but it steadily increases as speeds approach the speed of light until it becomes the dominant effect of trying to push things ever faster. Any space engineers attempting to break the light barrier would be frustrated by this effect, which would seem to work against their best efforts: the more power they build into their rocket, the heavier the rocket becomes at high speed, forever forbidding success.

Thus every object with mass has one fundamental 'rest mass', the mass we find it to have when it is at rest relative to us, but an endless series of larger 'relativistic masses', with the difference between the two determined by the speed at which the object is moving relative to us. Before we move on, remind yourself of what this 'difference in mass' really means: since the twin features of the phenomenon we call mass are its resistance to change in motion (the property of inertia) and its ability to create the force of gravity, then, as objects speed up, we find that it takes more of a push to change their motion by a given amount, and they exert a greater force of gravitational attraction on the things around them.

The other puzzles we mused upon earlier were connected to these twin properties of mass. We wondered 'Why should certain objects (that is, those with mass) resist changes in their motion – what makes them do so?' and 'Why and how do such objects give rise to the attractive force of gravity that surrounds them?'

Scientists have speculated on the first puzzle for centuries, and they continue to do so. It is the puzzle of the origin of inertia, for inertia is the name given to the tendency of objects with mass to resist changes in their motion. How and why does such resistance occur? Modern physicists are pretty happy with their understanding of how things start moving, or stop moving, or change their motion; but many are not at all happy with their understanding of how things resist such changes with their tendency to retain whatever motion they already have. To some, it seems a pointless question, but one possible answer is fascinating.

We may live in a universe which, on large scales, is completely symmetrical in terms of the distribution of matter and in which every place is surrounded by exactly the same amount of matter as any other place. At first sight, this might seem impossible, since a symmetrical universe might seem to imply a spherical one in which some places would be nearer the 'edge' of the sphere than others. That may well be a simplistic notion, however, due to our naive experience of only three dimensions of space. To appreciate how we may be deceived, imagine that we are flat creatures living on the surface of a perfectly smooth planet and aware of only the two dimensions of the flat surface. We would be bemused to discover that heading off in one direction would eventually bring us back to where we started. How can that be? we would ask, and would be puzzled to be told that our world is not truly flat, but that it curves back on itself slightly into the third dimension. This curvature, we are told, means that any point on the surface of our world is surrounded by an equal amount of the rest of our world in all directions. There is no edge – wherever we happen to be is equivalent to any other place, in terms of the amount of our world surrounding us.

Of course we are not really flat two-dimensional beings, we

are mighty three-dimensional ones who have no difficulty in seeing how a two-dimensional creature on the surface of a large sphere might not understand how that surface can 'bend back on itself' through another dimension. So we should not be too bemused to be told that our own three-dimensional space (four-dimensional spacetime) might be 'curved back on itself' through a dimension or dimensions not apparent to us, causing us to be surrounded on all sides by an equal expanse of universe, an equal number of galaxies and stars, regardless of where we happen to be at any time.

Let us accept that possibility for a moment, and then consider the effect of the force of gravity exerted by all these galaxies and their stars. The effect would average out so that it would be equal in all directions. So, superimposed on the unbalanced gravitational force we feel from the earth directly beneath us, there may be a gravitational pull on us by the rest of the universe that is equal in all directions. To change our motion we would need to fight against this all-encompassing gravitational force – we would need to fight against the pull of the rest of the universe! That, according to this line of reasoning, is the origin of inertia. Objects with mass tend to resist changes in their motion, and so tend to retain whatever form of motion they originally have, because to accelerate or decelerate they must counter the gravitational force of the stars and galaxies that surround them to equal extents in all directions. Next time you accelerate hard in your car, and feel yourself pressed against the back of your seat, reflect on the possibility that what is 'pulling' you back is the entire rest of the universe – an uncountable gathering of galaxies and their stars all reaching out with fingers of gravity that try to keep little you where you were!

This fascinating proposal about the origin of inertia is just that – a mere proposal which, although supported by some evidence, remains a matter of debate. It is, however, the best idea that physicists have come up with so far; and, like all good ideas in science, it simplifies our view of nature. It means that instead of wondering why some objects, the ones we say have mass, are associated with the property of inertia *and* the tendency to generate gravity, we simply need to worry about their tendency to generate gravity, for it is the gravitational pull of all other objects that makes any one object possess inertia. So now we have just that one puzzle about mass remaining (at least, of the puzzles I have chosen to draw attention to) – the puzzle of why and how objects with mass generate the force of gravity, and of what exactly *is* gravity. Considering possible answers will also reveal more about what mass actually is, but that puzzle is considered all on its own in chapter 4.

3 Forces

We are surrounded by things that move and change, in fact we are made from things that move and change. All things, from the galaxies and their stars to the tiniest sub-atomic particles within us, are moving and participating in changes. The movement and the changes occur because there are what physicists call 'forces' at work in the universe, forces which often exert simple pushes and pulls like those associated with the everyday meaning of the word force, but which can also bring about other more subtle effects.

Physicists often prefer to use the word 'interaction' instead of force, referring to 'the gravitational interaction' for example, rather than the gravitational force. The use of the term interaction emphasizes that some effects of forces are more subtle than mere pushes or pulls; and it also emphasizes the point that whenever one object exerts a force on some second object, the second object also exerts an equal and opposite force on the other. This effect is well known as Isaac Newton's law that 'for every action there is an equal and opposite reaction', which simply means that the things we call forces are due to mutual *interactions* between the objects concerned.

At a first glance, it appears that many different forces operate in the world and the universe at large. There is the force of the wind and of the sea, the mighty force of earthquakes and volcanoes, the force of water rushing over waterfalls, the force of a meteorite striking the earth, the force of freezing water opening up cracks in solid rock. There is the force within the muscles of living things, allowing them to hold themselves up against the force of gravity and to move about and lift things up and push them around. There is the explosive force of petrol which pushes at the pistons of car engines and compels the cars to move, the force of electricity causing light bulbs to glow and electrical appliances to work, the force of magnetism making some metals jump towards magnets, the force of sound waves setting up vibrations in your ear . . . The list continues, but it conceals a wonderful simplicity. As you examine diverse forces in detail you discover unity beneath the diversity. You discover that only a few forces operating in different situations create the illusion of many different forces.

There are, in fact, no more than four forces responsible for all of the pushing and pulling and changing that occurs in Nature. These are called the four 'fundamental forces' and are known as the gravitational force, the electromagnetic force, the weak nuclear force and the strong nuclear force.

Gravity is the fundamental force we are most familiar with. It is a force attracting all objects with mass towards one another, pulling together apples and the earth, the moon and the earth, planets and their stars, and pulling stars towards one another into galaxies. The space through which a force such as gravity acts is said to be occupied by a 'force field', so that every object with mass is associated with its surrounding field of gravitational force. You will discover in chapter 7, however, that scientist's views about the nature of such force fields are more subtle than might at first be supposed.

The next most familiar of the fundamental forces is the electromagnetic force, responsible for both electric and magnetic effects. Some objects, ultimately some sub-atomic particles such as the familiar protons and electrons within atoms, are pushed and pulled by one another's presence in a manner that indicates that a seemingly quite different force from gravity is at work. For one thing, this force can push some things apart, be 'repulsive' in other words, while gravity is only 'attractive', pulling things together. Objects which produce and respond to this force are said to do so because they carry a certain amount of 'electric charge', just as objects that produce and respond to gravity possess mass (which we could call 'mass charge' if we wished). Nobody really knows for sure what electric charge is – it is simply a name given to a property of objects which generate and feel the force known as the electric force.

As most people know, there are two opposite types of electric charge, known as 'positive' (+) and 'negative' (−), and the basic rule of movement under the influence of the electric force is that objects of opposite charge are attracted towards one another, while those carrying the same sign of charge are repelled from one another. Thus positive charge and negative charge are attracted towards one another, while two or more positives will repel one another, as will two or more negatives. The force of attraction or repulsion between objects carrying electrical charge is responsible for almost all of the forces we experience directly, other than gravity. The force that strains to pull a rubber band back into shape, the force of a muscle lifting a weight and the force of a chemical explosion are just three examples of everyday forces that are really due to the electric force pushing and pulling at the electrically charged particles within the objects concerned. The way in which one force can create these diverse effects will become clearer later, when we consider the basic nature of chemistry and life.

So much for what has been called the 'electric' force; where does the 'magnetic' aspect of the electromagnetic force come from? It used to be thought that the effects of the electric force and the phenomenon of magnetism were caused by two distinct electric and magnetic forces, but in the 1850s James Clerk Maxwell demonstrated that both were distinct aspects of one 'electromagnetic' force. It turns out that magnetic fields, or in other words the force fields created by objects we call magnets, are generated by *the motion* of objects carrying electric charges. So the force that swings a compass needle round to North, and the force of static electricity that causes a rubbed comb to pick up dust and pieces of paper, are different manifestations of one fundamental electromagnetic force.

The information about the electromagnetic force given above makes it easy for us to realize why Nature needs at least one other force in order for our world to make sense. Many people are familiar with the basic structure of the particles of matter known as atoms, in which positively charged particles called protons cluster together into a tiny central 'nucleus'.

Some force must hold these protons together, because otherwise the electric force would be expected to push them apart
since they all carry the same type of charge, namely positive.
The force which, at short ranges, can overcome this repulsive
effect is known as 'the strong nuclear force'. This strong force
is also felt by the electrically neutral particles called neutrons,
and it binds protons and neutrons together into the nuclei of
atoms.

The last of nature's forces is the more obscure 'weak nuclear
force', responsible for some subtle transformations within the
nuclei of atoms associated with the emission of 'beta' radio-
activity. A neutron within an atom can sometimes break down
into a proton, which stays in the atom, and a fast-moving
electron which flies away from the atom as soon as it is formed.
Beta rays are composed of streams of these released electrons
coming out of a substance. The weak nuclear force is
responsible for the initial transformation of neutrons which
generates beta rays.

In fact, this weak nuclear force now appears to be almost
certainly another subtle manifestation of the force responsible
for electricity and magnetism. Increasingly, we see the term
'electromagnetic force' being replaced by 'electroweak' force
(although 'electromagnetoweak' might seem more sensible), in
recognition of this apparent unity.

So scientists aiming to describe and utilize the pushing and
pulling and changing powers of Nature have probably only
three fundamental forces to deal with, the gravitational,
electroweak and strong nuclear forces, together with the
mysterious charges associated with each force and which
cause specific things to feel the effects of each force.

Things might well prove to be even simpler than that. We
have already seen how the apparently different electric and
magnetic forces turned out to be separate aspects of the one
electromagnetic force; and then how the weak nuclear force
appears to be just a further manifestation of the same force,
now called the electroweak force. That process of discovery has
'united' three seemingly distinct forces into one, and the
search for further underlying unity continues. At present,
physicists have good reason to believe that the strong nuclear

force may fit into the unification as well, meaning that one fundamental force may be responsible for the superficially distinct strong nuclear, weak nuclear and electromagnetic forces. There may even be only the one universal 'superforce', if gravity turns out also to fit into the unification, as some physicists suggest.

Such ideas of further unification of the forces are speculations at the moment rather than firm facts; but even the current state of play reveals a pleasing and stunning simplicity of forces at the heart of all change. It seems that at most there are only four, probably only three, and perhaps just two or one, fundamental forces at work in the universe. The interplay between these forces and objects with corresponding charges is responsible for all of the pushing and pulling and changing that makes things happen.

4   Gravity

We are so used to gravity that it is easy to forget that it is there, yet it is what holds us on our world, the earth, and what holds the earth in comfortable proximity to the life-giving energy source we call the sun, and what holds the sun and all other stars in the vast assemblies of stars we call galaxies. If gravity were suddenly 'switched off', your first attempt to walk would propel you slowly but inexorably away from the earth towards an endless journey through the vacuum of space; the earth itself would go careering away from the sun until that sun became just another distant star in the cold sky; and the entire structure of the cosmos would gradually drift into unconnected loneliness. So the force of gravity is both comfortably familiar to us and fundamental for our existence; yet gravity is another natural phenomenon which looks utterly different when viewed in the light of the insights of Albert Einstein. It is another natural phenomenon whose true nature may be very different from what everyday experience would suggest.

Albert Einstein's ideas about the unity of space and time, discussed in chapter 1, are known as his 'special' theory of relativity (or theory of 'special relativity'), since they describe space and time as observed by people moving in a special way relative to one another, special because they must be moving at a constant velocity relative to one another. They must not, in other words, be undergoing any *acceleration*. When this condition is met, Einstein demonstrated that exactly the same physical laws will apply to everyone, and they will all find that moving clocks run slower than their own, and that distances are contracted in the direction of motion of objects moving relative to themselves. Einstein's next task, however, was to consider the position of people whose relative motion did not meet the special criterion of no acceleration. In particular, was it possible to devise a theory of physics, a description of events, in other words, that would apply equally to all people, regardless of how they were moving, accelerating or decelerating? By 1915 he was ready to announce his results, in what became known as his 'general' theory of relativity.

The first big step in his reasoning was to make clear a link between the phenomenon of acceleration and that of gravity, a link which is known as the 'principle of equivalence' between acceleration and gravity, meaning that the effects of acceleration and gravity are the same. To appreciate this, consider the example Einstein used himself: imagine you are in a windowless box far out in space where the forces of gravity are so weak that you consider there to be no gravity at all. You are floating around in a 'weightless' condition, waiting for something to happen. Over a period of time, for some reason unknown to you, you begin to feel your weight again. You fall gently towards one wall of your box, and feel yourself become heavier until everything seems just as it would if the box had gently returned to the surface of earth. You can stand up, jump up and down, throw things in the air and watch them fall; but you cannot climb up to the roof or float around freely as you once could. How can this change be explained? One obvious explanation would be that your box had come under the influence of a gravitational field, since your experience on earth has taught you that what you are experiencing now is just what life in a gravitational field feels like. This might be some new gravitational field, or your box might really have gently returned to earth. There is another equally plausible possibility, though – your box could have begun to *accelerate*.

We all know what it feels like to be accelerated as we sit in an aircraft rushing down a runway, or even simply sit in an accelerating car. Acceleration causes us to feel a force that apparently pulls us 'back' in the opposite direction to the acceleration. So an appropriate degree of steady acceleration in a box free of the complicating effect of the gravity of earth could make you feel pulled towards one wall of the box by exactly the same amount as any given gravitational force. This is a great insight – the effects of gravity and acceleration are the same, or, in other words, the effects of gravity and acceleration are 'equivalent'.

How did this equivalence help Einstein develop his theories about gravity? It led him to describe the effects of gravity, using the same methods as could describe the effects of motion, particularly accelerated motion.

If we watch an object moving past us with no acceleration, with a constant velocity in other words, we find that it is moving in a steady direction through the four-dimensional world of spacetime. If it then begins to accelerate, however, then its motion through spacetime becomes curved. The origin of this curvature is explained in chapter 1: as the object's speed changes relative to us, it undergoes a sort of 'rotation' in spacetime. The direction in which it is travelling through spacetime constantly changes as long as it is accelerating, and anything moving while constantly changing direction is moving in a curve.

So much for things that are accelerating; what about things that are experiencing the force of gravity? If the effects of acceleration and of standing still in a gravitational field are equivalent, then anyone standing still in a gravitational field must be moving in a curve through spacetime. How can anyone apparently standing still in the three dimensions of space be moving in a curve through spacetime? They are always moving through time, of course, and therefore moving through spacetime even when standing still, so they could be following a curved path through spacetime if the spacetime itself were somehow curved or distorted in the gravitational field. This is Einstein's astonishing conclusion: gravity corresponds to a distortion (curving, warping, twisting – call it what you like) of the very fabric of spacetime. What we call a gravitational 'field' appears in fact to be just a region of spacetime that has become distorted by the presence of matter – by the presence of objects with mass. So, according to Einstein's general theory of relativity, gravity and the apparent gravitational force disappear into mere distortion of spacetime. When we say that objects with mass generate a gravitational field, we should really say that the fundamental feature of objects with mass is that they distort the structure of spacetime. Gravity is dead, long live curved spacetime!

This might appear to contradict the discussion of the previous chapter, which described gravity as a definite force pulling objects with mass towards one another. This apparent contradiction reveals something important about the nature of science, and how scientific knowledge develops. It is true that the effects of gravity can be very accurately *described* as due to some pulling force between objects with mass, but it seems equally true that the effects of gravity can be *described* as due to objects with mass distorting the spacetime they are embedded in. It is perfectly acceptable in science to have two different descriptions of the one real phenomenon in use at the same time. Each one is described as a 'model' of reality, and sometimes two seemingly distinct models can be used quite legitimately to describe the actual reality as seen from different points of view. The idea of gravity as a simple pulling force is the older model of gravity, and it works very well. The idea of gravity as due to the curving of spacetime is a newer model, and it too works very well, sometimes better. The newer model may well completely replace the older one, as tends to happen quite often in science, but at the moment the true nature of gravity is still the subject of some debate. That too is perfectly normal and acceptable. Science cannot be described as finished business. It is a field of great activity, change and not a little uncertainty and confusion. As time goes by the descriptions science offers of reality – the models in use – evolve as they approach ever closer to the true nature of reality; but few physicists would yet claim that any of their models match the reality exactly. This is an important point to bear in mind as you read this book. It is a progress report on science's developing view of Nature, not a final summary of a finished job.

So, at present, physicists still talk about gravity as a conventional pulling force, when it suits them to do so, but when they become concerned with the true detailed nature of the phenomenon then they prefer the model in which gravitational effects are due to the curvature of spacetime associated with objects possessing mass. That is what they increasingly feel to be a truer representation of the reality.

So, if gravity is due to the curving of spacetime, why do things fall towards the earth? Why does the earth circle the sun? Why are stars like the sun drawn together and held in unimaginably large galaxies? In the language of the previous chapter all these effects can be attributed to the 'force' of gravity, pulling all objects with mass towards all other objects. Einstein's view of gravity, however, explains them as due to the natural movement of things through the distorted world of curved spacetime. A ball released from our hand falls towards the earth because spacetime 'kinks inwards' towards the earth, and as the ball moves through spacetime it must inevitably follow the kinks. The earth circling the sun appears to us to be moving in an endlessly repeating curved path, but that is only because we cannot directly see that spacetime itself is curved around the sun, so that the earth is in fact moving along the shortest route, i.e. in a 'straight line', through curved spacetime.

The 'force' of gravity appears to have slipped from our grasp, replaced by the baffling concept of objects simply moving through mysteriously curved spacetime. This seems difficult and puzzling to us because it bears no relation to everyday experience, but it actually makes the concept of gravity rather simpler by allowing it to be described merely in terms of the *geometry* of the universal 'fabric' we call spacetime.

Some physicists at the forefront of current research are trying to see if all forces, and not just gravity, can be incorporated into a similar but extended geometrical plan. Can all forces, in other words, merely be viewed as the result of objects moving in shortest-path 'straight lines' through a spacetime that is warped and twisted in ways we find difficult to comprehend? Considerable progress has been made with such ideas, and they all involve a universe with several 'unseen' dimensions of spacetime which are not apparent to us directly, but only indirectly through the phenomena we label as 'forces'. If you follow the progress of science through the next few years and decades, be prepared to see the development and success of a comprehensive 'theory of everything', in which all objects and events are seen to be manifestations of the complex geometry of a spacetime with many more dimensions (11 is the current best guess!) than are recognized at present. At the moment several different candidate theories of everything are being developed and set in competition against one another, but none has yet proved triumphant. The final triumph of theoretical physics might emerge from this arena soon. What Einstein discovered about gravity, the most familiar of Nature's forces, may eventually lead us to a comprehensive and unifying understanding of all forces in terms of the shifting geometry of spacetime.

5   Energy

What do we need to construct the universe? What is the basic shopping list for creation? The earlier chapters of this book have considered five phenomena that would be right at the top of the list: space, time, matter, force and charge. The more knowledgeable and concise shopper would write just four: spacetime, matter, force and charge. But there is still something vital missing from the list: the phenomenon known as 'energy'.

Unlike many scientific terms, energy is a word in everyday use. We may talk of not having the energy to get up in the morning, of the generation of electrical energy in power stations, of the consumption of the energy of petrol by our cars, and of the energy of food by ourselves, and so on; but such talk uses the term rather loosely, and to understand the idea of energy properly we need to be careful about what it really means.

As we study physics at school most of us encounter the standard definition of energy as 'the capacity to do work'. That certainly sets us on the way to understanding energy, but it does merely define energy in terms of another word used rather loosely in everyday language. It begs the question, what do we mean by work?

One common way of expressing the scientific idea of work is to say that 'work is done when a weight is raised or when a process occurs which could, in principle, be used to raise a weight.' This definition implies that raising a certain weight (1 kilogram, for example) through a certain height (1 metre, for example) can be used as a standard measure of work, against which all other processes involving work can be measured; but what does it imply about the actual process of work itself, and therefore about energy itself?

It tells us that work is done when an object with mass is moved *against* the pull of the gravitational force (or moved through a path other than its natural path through curved spacetime, if we adopt the description of gravity outlined in chapter 4). The realization that work involves fighting against a force is the crucial insight into what is really meant by work and energy. In our definition of work, the gravitational force is merely used as the most familiar representative of the fundamental forces. We could just as easily have said that 'work is done when a positively charged object is pulled away from a negatively charged object, or when a process occurs which could, in principle, be used to pull a positively charged object away from a negatively charged object.' So we can broaden the definition of work into 'work is done when something is moved against the effect (such as the push or the pull) of a fundamental force.'

Armed with this definition of work, we can examine more closely the meaning of energy, so far defined as just the capacity to do work. If energy is the capacity to do work, and work is done when something moves against the effect of a fundamental force, clearly energy must be 'the capacity to bring about movement against the effect of a fundamental force'. In loose descriptive terms we can think of the phenomenon of energy as some sort of 'force resistance' or even 'antiforce', where 'force' refers to one of the fundamental forces.

Energy is a property stored within, or embodied in, any part of the universe which we distinguish by calling it 'a system'. A system can be any part of Nature we choose, from something as small as an atom, through assemblies such as living cells, living organisms, machines and geological structures, up to entire planets, stars, galaxies and even the entire universe itself. Systems containing lots of energy are often loosely referred to as 'high energy' systems, or high energy 'states'; while those with less energy are 'low energy'; although such statements clearly discuss energy in relative terms rather than absolute quantities.

A rock perched on some ledge high up a mountainside is a simple example of a high energy state, since in being stuck much higher from the surface of the earth than it might be, its position clearly embodies some defiance of the fundamental force of gravity. Another way of describing such 'defiance' is to point out that the gravitational force is clearly 'set up' ready to force the rock downwards, should a subtle change in conditions allow it to. If the rock were to be jolted off of its ledge and allowed to fall, it would end up stationary on the ground in a lower energy state than its previous one. On the ground, the gravitational force is no longer 'set up' to make the rock fall, and the position of the rock clearly defies gravity less; but what has happened to the energy it has lost? Has it gone somewhere else or has it disappeared? The answer is that it has gone somewhere else. It has been *transferred* to another system or systems. In the simplest case the energy lost will be transferred into the ground when the rock hits the ground. The impact will cause the particles (atoms, molecules and ions) of the ground to move about more quickly, and, as is discussed more fully below, all movement is a form of energy. So, as the rock hits the ground it pushes against the particles of the ground, which in turn push against the rock. This causes the rock to stop falling, but also makes the particles in the ground 'bounce around' more vigorously as they are disturbed by the collision with the rock. The energy originally possessed by the rock is then steadily dissipated throughout the ground due to collisions between the particles in the ground. The energy originally stored in the position of the rock ends up being stored in the more vigorous movement of the particles of the ground.

Transfers of energy such as this are a fundamental feature of all changes, and energy transfer is all that can happen to energy for, to quote a well-known dictum of school science, 'energy cannot be created or destroyed, merely redistributed.' That bold classic statement will be modified somewhat later, when we consider the link between energy and mass, but in a slightly modified form it remains a fundamental dictum of modern science. There is a certain amount of energy in the universe, and that energy merely becomes redistributed during natural changes. One interesting and subtle twist to that idea, however, is that the 'certain amount' of energy in the universe may be zero overall, since some types of energy can be described mathematically as 'positive' and others as 'negative', with equal amounts of positive and negative energy cancelling out when the universe as a whole is considered (see page 65 for a fuller discussion).

Having looked at a very simple high energy system, and observed how it might change to a lower energy system, we should check that the energy contained in the system meets the requirement of being able to do work, such as raising a weight. If we arranged for our rock to fall onto one end of a seesaw with someone sitting on the other end, clearly the arrival of the rock could raise the person upwards, perhaps only a little, perhaps a lot, depending on the size of the rock, the extent of its fall and the person's weight. Whatever the magnitude of the effect, the fall of the rock certainly has the capacity to do work. It does the work of raising the person on the seesaw in defiance of the force of gravity, while the rock's own defiance of gravity disappears. So the energy originally possessed by the rock due to its height up the mountainside is transferred into the higher position of the person on the seesaw.

It is fairly easy to see why a rock perched high up a mountainside is a high energy system. In other cases things are not so obvious. Chemical fuels such as coal, oil, gas and petrol are other examples of systems which are relatively high energy ones, but the origin of their energy is rather more subtle. They contain energy due to the precise arrangement of their chemical components, particularly the arrangement of the negatively charged sub-atomic particles called electrons and the positively charged sub-atomic particles called protons. The energy content and energy changes of chemicals are considered fully in later chapters, but in the meantime consider this simple generalization: chemicals contain energy because the arrangement of their electrons and protons involves some defiance of the electromagnetic force (the one that pulls opposite charges together and forces identical charges apart), and also because their constituent particles are in motion.

A recurring theme is emerging: high energy states are associated with objects whose *positions* involve some defiance of the effect of a fundamental force, or with objects which are in *motion*, or some combination of these two effects. Two distinct types of energy can be distinguished here: energy associated with position and energy associated with motion. These are known in science as 'potential energy' and 'kinetic energy' respectively, terms which we should examine a little more closely.

The energy objects possess by virtue of their positions is known as 'potential energy', because these objects clearly have the potential to do work if their positions change to ones that involve less defiance of a fundamental force. Thus, rocks high up in a gravitational field, or positively charged objects some distance away from negatively charged ones, are two examples of systems containing potential energy due to objects having positions which defy the fundamental gravitational or electro-magnetic forces.

Anything that is moving has a certain amount of kinetic energy, depending on how fast it is moving and how massive it is. To understand why moving objects possess some energy as a result of their movement, consider the very simple example of a ball rolling along a flat surface for a while, and then encountering an uphill slope. The movement of the ball will take it steadily onwards until it encounters the slope. To begin with the movement will propel the ball up the slope, although the ball will slow as it rises. The ball, of course, possesses some weight, so in rising up the slope a weight is being raised – the criterion for the performance of work. So the movement of the ball can serve to do some work, such as raising the weight of the ball itself, and thus the ball must possess a certain amount of energy associated with its movement.

The kinetic energy of motion and the potential energy of position are the two fundamental and *interconvertible* forms of energy. They are interconverted as our ball climbs its slope. As the ball moves up the slope its kinetic energy of motion decreases, but its potential energy increases since the ball is rising upwards in defiance of gravity. Eventually, the upward movement ceases, at which point all of the initial kinetic energy has been converted into potential energy. Unless there is some mechanism to keep the ball in this new position, it will immediately begin to fall again, with its potential energy being converted back into kinetic energy as it moves off in the opposite direction, from which it came. A similar slope on the opposite side of the system, however, could ensure that the interconversion between kinetic and potential energy continued. If we could get rid of the forces of friction between the ball and the surface it is rolling on, and avoid the problem of air resistance by allowing the ball to roll in a vacuum, the ball would roll back and forth forever, first up one slope, then down and across to and up the second slope, and so on, in an endless cycle of energy conversion – kinetic to potential to kinetic to potential . . .: perpetual motion!

In the real world, of course, friction and air resistance would gradually bring the motion to a halt as the ball's energy is dissipated away into the surface it is rolling upon and the air around it. Such 'dissipation' of energy due to friction and air resistance (which is really just friction between the ball and the air) is ultimately due to collisions between the atoms of the ball and those of the surface it is rolling on and of the air. In these collisions, some of the atoms of the surface and the air will be jolted into moving faster, and therefore with more energy, when they collide with and push against the atoms of the ball. The ball, in turn, will be slowed by this process, since the atoms of the surface and the air will push against the ball, in the opposite direction to its motion, as the ball tries to move over the surface and through the air.

We have now defined and discussed energy in outline, but there are surprises in store as we investigate the phenomenon of energy more fully. Albert Einstein's insights were not restricted to overturning classical views of space, time and gravity; he also turned his attention to energy, and in the process revolutionized understanding of both energy and mass.

Recall from chapter 2 that as objects speed up they get more massive, and therefore heavier, which was explained as a consequence of the fact that nothing can be accelerated beyond the speed of light. We imagined an object being subjected to a series of equal pushes, with each push resulting in less of an increase in velocity than the previous one, and causing a greater increase in the object's mass. Now it takes energy to give an object a push. As we push at and accelerate an object we are doing 'work' on it, and energy, remember, is defined as the ability to do work. So each push on a spaceship, for example, provided by burning a certain fixed amount of rocket fuel, will supply an equal amount of energy to the spaceship. What does this energy do? At first, its most obvious effect is to increase the speed of the spaceship, but we know that it must also increase the spaceship's mass. As the ship accelerates ever closer to the speed of light, so the increase in mass becomes the dominant effect – energy is being supplied to the spaceship and is serving to increase its mass.

This was the logical basis of what is perhaps Einstein's most celebrated discovery: the phenomenon we call energy can create the phenomenon we call mass. There is clearly a deep link between energy and the mass of matter. Einstein put it in words, like this: 'the mass of a body is a measure of its energy content'; and in symbolic form like this:

$$E = mc^2$$

This is the most famous equation of science, indicating that the energy (E) of an object (measured in units called Joules) is equal to its mass (m, measured in kilograms) multiplied by the speed of light (c, in metres per second) and then all multiplied by the speed of light again (in other words $E = m \times c \times c$). The precise units and figures do not matter if we wish simply to grasp the principles. The central principle is that energy can serve to create mass, and, conversely, mass can serve to create energy. A more accurate way of expressing the link is to say that all energy also has a certain amount of mass, and all mass has a certain amount of energy, with the amounts being determined by the equation $E = mc^2$.

This relationship between mass and energy is not simply an arcane principle of physics, it is the relationship that lies behind the energy released from nuclear weapons, nuclear power stations and the nuclear fusion reactor we call the sun.

In a nuclear explosion some matter is destroyed to release a corresponding amount of energy (as heat, light, and in other forms). In the heart of a nuclear power plant the release of the energy locked up in particles of matter proceeds in a more controlled manner, releasing the heat that is used to boil water to create the steam that turns the turbine blades of electricity generators. In the sun, atoms of matter are fused together to produce new ones possessing a bit less mass than the original ones, with the corresponding energy being released as heat and light and other radiations.

In summary, energy and mass, instead of being two totally distinct phenomena, are intimately related: the mass of a body is a measure of its energy content, so mass, and therefore matter, can be regarded as a form of 'locked up energy'. Locked up, but waiting to be released.

Let's look back at our 'shopping list for creation' briefly, before we move on. To spacetime, matter, force and charge, we can now add energy. But we have just seen that energy and the mass which is the distinguishing feature of matter are best regarded as two aspects of the same phenomenon, a phenomenon which has been variously described as mass-energy, or matter-energy, or even massergy or mattergy. So our shopping list becomes abbreviated once more, into spacetime, mass-energy, force and charge. Four ingredients to make a universe, including all its life! The remainder of this book will explore how these ingredients actually do mix together to make the universe and its life, and we shall even encounter possibilities for abbreviating the ingredients list further.

6 Particles

People with a tendency to philosophize about science can spend a lot of time agonizing about the relationship between the whole of something and its parts. Is the whole the 'mere' sum of its parts? Is the whole much more than the sum of its parts? Does something mysterious, magical, mystical, occur when the parts aggregate and interact to generate the whole? What is rarely challenged is the notion that it is, at least for some purposes, useful to regard large structures in the universe – 'wholes' – as composed of many smaller parts. So how far can we go in the process of breaking things down into ever smaller parts? The simple answer of school science is that we can keep on breaking until we reach the tiny entities known as particles, although some particles can be broken down into smaller 'fundamental' particles. Nobody should be in awe of the term particles, it really just means small parts. Scientists use it, however, to describe a particular series of small parts of the universe, the largest of which are called molecules, followed, as we move downwards in size, by atoms, protons, neutrons, quarks and electrons, to name just a few of the more familiar particles. In this chapter we must consider what such particles are, what the differences between them are, what similarities they share and why they are so important and influential.

The easiest sort of particles for non-scientists to comprehend are particles of matter – in other words, the little bits of matter that one eventually arrives at by splitting big bits of matter into smaller bits. In principle, for example (although it would be difficult to achieve in practice), one could take a lump of the metal iron, smash it into small fragments, smash the small fragments into smaller ones, and continue smashing up ever smaller fragments until one obtained a collection of iron atoms. These are the smallest bits of a lump of iron which can still behave chemically like iron: which can participate, in other words, in the same chemical reactions as larger lumps of iron. The atoms are not indivisible 'fundamental' particles, however, since they can be split up into three types of smaller 'sub-atomic' particles known as protons, neutrons and electrons. If we split up an iron atom, we would find 26 protons, 26 electrons and probably 30 neutrons (the number of neutrons in an atom can vary). As far as is known the electrons could be split no further, they are true fundamental particles; but each proton and neutron is composed of three smaller fundamental particles known as quarks (although so far no-one has split them up into free quarks and such splitting may well be impossible).

So, particles of matter such as atoms, protons, neutrons and electrons are just little bits of matter; but what are they really? It is tempting to suppose that they must be similar to what we call matter in our everyday world, only much smaller. So it is similarly tempting to suppose that particles are hard little objects like tiny pool balls or billiard balls. Unfortunately, that is hopelessly naive. To gain a true insight into the structure of Nature we must shed most of our 'common-sense' simplistic preconceptions about Nature. We have already been forced to abandon, or at least adapt, our everyday notions of space and time and gravity. As we investigate the true nature of particles we will need to abandon our everyday notions of matter. In our everyday world, matter is nice sensible solid dependable stuff. You can slap your hand against the solid matter of a wall, roll the hard matter of a stone in your hand, and feel the heavy solidity of your own matter as you settle into an armchair; but the solidity and security of matter evaporates as you investigate it in ever finer detail. Eventually (in chapter 7) we will find it slips from our grasp into somewhat ghostly abstraction. This should not discourage us from attempting to learn more about the particles of matter. As soon as matter begins to puzzle and bemuse us, we are beginning to appreciate its true nature. As a start, we must begin to think about particles, including particles of matter, as 'phenomena' rather than as tiny hard balls. Particles of matter are not tiny hard balls of matter, even though they often behave as if they are, but are intriguing and still not properly understood phenomena found in the world of spacetime.

Some other particles cannot even be described as particles of matter, because they have no 'rest mass' – that is, they have no mass at all when they are stationary. Some people are tempted to query how they can be there at all, if they have no mass, but, remembering to think about all particles as *phenomena*, we must try to appreciate that particles with no rest mass are real phenomena, just as subtle things like opinions and trends and inflation rates and changes are real phenomena in our everyday world, even though we cannot grasp hold of them and roll them about in our hands.

We will discover more about particles with no mass soon, but as our feet begin to slip on the slope down to the dark depths of theoretical physics and philosophy, let us step back and try to regain our balance by learning more about the characteristics that make particles what they are.

Most particles can be described by listing six main characteristics, or 'vital statistics'. The first vital statistic of a particle is its mass – a measure of how much matter it corresponds to, how strong a gravitational field it creates, how heavy it is, and, according to Einstein, how much curvature of spacetime is associated with it.

The second vital statistic is its electric charge – is it positively charged, negatively charged, or not electrically charged at all; and if it does have electric charge, how much does it have? Another way of answering the same question is to say whether or not the particle 'feels' the electromagnetic force, and if so in what way and to what extent.

The mass of a particle tells us about its link to the gravitational force, the electric charge tells us about its link to the electromagnetic force; but there are two other forces, the strong and the weak nuclear forces, that we need to know about as well. So vital statistics numbers three and four are the size and nature of the particle's 'strong charge' (the extent to which it feels the strong force, if at all, which technically involves a phenomenon known to physicists as 'colour'), and the size and nature of its 'weak charge' (the extent to which it feels the weak force, if at all).

Only two other pieces of information are required to summarize the main characteristics of a particle. The first is its lifetime, a measure of how long it can be expected to last. This is best measured in terms of the 'half-life' of the particle, which is the time taken for one half of a large number of the particles to decay into something else. This rather indirect measure of lifetime is required because, much like our own lives, the lifetime of any individual particle is not strictly determined and cannot be precisely predicted in advance; but the variations in lifetimes average out within a large sample to yield a very precise half-life, which can range from much less than one trillionth of a second to many billions of years. Some particles appear to last for so long that they are often referred to as being 'stable', meaning that their lifetime can be regarded as infinite.

The final vital statistic of a particle is known as its spin, which can be thought of very loosely as a measure of the extent to which it is spinning on its axis. This is, however, only a rather inaccurate way of visualizing a considerably more subtle phenomenon.

So mass, electric charge, strong charge, weak charge, half-life and spin are the six vital statistics of particles, giving us, in other words, information about any particle's relationship with the gravitational force, the electromagnetic force, the strong force, the weak force, how long it lasts and the way in which its properties change as it moves through spacetime. There are other things that we must say about some particles in order to describe them fully, but these are the six main things we must first know.

A particle's vital statistics are usually related in the following way: The mass can be quoted in 'atomic mass units', a unit which conveniently places the masses of protons and neutrons at very close to 1; or the mass can be given in terms of the energy associated with the mass as determined by the equation $E = mc^2$. Remember, also, that each particle will have a fundamental rest mass, and a series of larger masses corresponding to its mass when moving at certain velocities. The electric charge is quoted in terms of the charge on a proton, +1, or an electron, −1, so that any particle will have a charge of zero if it does not feel the electric force, or plus or minus some multiple or fraction of +1 and −1 if it does. In a brief summary of particles, it is usual simply to state whether or not they feel or 'couple with' the strong force and the weak force. Half-lives can be quoted simply in seconds or years, while spins are given as multiples of a fundamental amount of spin described as ½, although spins can be + or −, corresponding to 'spinning' in opposite directions.

The subject of this chapter is particles in general, not any individual particles in particular. You will meet various individual particles of matter in later chapters, where such vital statistics about them as are relevant will be given. In the meantime, we must consider one characteristic that allows all particles to be placed in one of two fundamental categories.

According to modern physical theory, the forces that push and pull at particles of matter are themselves the effect of the *exchange* of another set of particles which actually 'carry' or 'bring about the effect of' the forces. Consider two electrons, the well-known particles of matter that possess negative electrical charge. Two electrons close to one another are forced apart due to the repulsive effect of the electromagnetic force. Modern physical theory says that this movement is brought about by the *exchange* of force-carrying particles between the electrons. So for each fundamental force, there must be one or more corresponding force-carrying or 'messenger' particles which travel between the particles responding to the force and which actually bring about the response. The carrier particles of the electromagnetic force are called photons, and are matched by 'gluons' which carry the strong force, 'gravitons' which carry the gravitational force (or are responsible for the curvature of spacetime associated with gravity, if we use the curvature description of gravity), and particles known simply as W and Z which carry the weak force. You will find more about these force-carrying particles in chapter 7, but for the meantime just realize that there are two great classes of particles: those which are the force carriers (and which all belong to a class of particles known as 'bosons'); and those particles of matter that are influenced by the force carriers.

There is a pleasing simplicity to be found at the heart of the particles which feel but do not carry the forces. It is that all such particles of matter are constructed out of four basic particles. Two of these particles are known as 'quarks', and specifically as the 'up' quark and the 'down' quark; while the other two are called 'leptons' and comprise the familiar electron and its much less familiar sibling the 'electron neutrino'.

So to construct our world we need the particles listed in table 6.1. Other particles exist, but all can be rationalized as composites of these basic or fundamental types. A proton, for example, consists of two up quarks and a down quark, a neutron consists of two down quarks and an up quark, and so on . . . . The much larger atoms and molecules, which are the particles most people are familiar with, are composed of varying numbers of protons, neutrons and electrons. We will be returning to consider the structure and behaviour of atoms and molecules in some detail when we begin to look at the basic nature of chemistry and biology (from chapter 9 onwards), rather than of fundamental physics.

There is one final complication: the basic set of two quarks and two leptons shown in table 6.1 is actually matched by two further generations of similar particles which can be created artificially in high energy particle accelerators, but which are not components of everyday matter. The second generation consists of a 'charmed quark' and 'strange quark', and a 'muon' and 'muon-neutrino'. The third generation consists of the 'top quark' and 'bottom quark' along with a 'tauon' and 'tauon-neutrino'. The names mean very little, they are just labels chosen for often rather flippant reasons. The main difference between members of the second and third generations and those of the first is that the second- and third-generation particles are heavier than their everyday relatives; and if we are only interested in the structure of everyday matter in the world around us we can forget about the higher generations entirely. The world around us can be understood

Table 6.1 *The particles found in the everyday world around us, which make up matter and mediate the forces of Nature.*

Particle		Rest mass (in 'atomic mass units')	Electric charge	Comments
Quarks	'Up' quark	approx. 0.327	$+\frac{2}{3}$	Many other particles are composed of quarks. Protons and neutrons, for example, each contain three quarks. The quarks are held together by the strong nuclear force
	'Down' quark	approx. 0.327	$-\frac{1}{3}$	
Leptons	Electron	0.000545	-1	Electrons combine with protons and neutrons, composed of quarks, to make up everyday stable matter
	Electron-neutrino	Less than 0.00000005	0	Electron-neutrinos are very abundant particles but, due to their tiny mass and lack of electric charge, they hardly interact with everyday matter
Bosons (force carriers)	Graviton	0	0	Responsible for the gravitational force
	Photon	0	0	Responsible for the electromagnetic force
	W^+, W^- and Z^0	approx. 550 each	$\begin{cases} W^+ = +1 \\ W^- = -1 \\ Z^0 = 0 \end{cases}$	Responsible for the weak nuclear force
	Gluons	0	0	Responsible for the strong nuclear force

in terms of four fundamental particles – the up and down quarks, the electron and the electron-neutrino, along with the force-carrying photons, gluons, gravitons and W and Z particles.

As you look around what has been called the 'particle zoo' meeting many exotic creatures with unfamiliar names and properties, you need to retain in your mind the central principles and simplicities of the particle world:

> Particles are best regarded as distinct phenomena found in the universe which often have rather subtle properties unlike everyday 'solid' objects like rocks and stones. By abandoning the view of particles as tiny hard spheres we make a great advance in our understanding of the micro-world. For one thing, particles are not immutable, they can be annihilated into pure energy just as they can be created out of nothing but energy, they exist for a while and then can either return to pure energy or can 'decay' into other types of particles. It is as if the 'spacetime fabric of the universe' whatever that is, can 'twist' itself up into many different guises which we call different particles, and it can just as readily untwist itself and make the particles disappear. Each type of particle has a different set of 'vital statistics' from other types – different mass, charge, spin etc. – and these statistics, or characteristics, are what determine what they do and what happens to them. The names we know the particles by are irrelevant; what they can do, in other words their characteristics, is all that matters.

The idea of the 'spacetime fabric of the universe' becoming 'twisted' into the different particles is not just colourful analogy. As we saw on page 29, there is a branch of theoretical physics which is attempting to explain everything, including all particles and all forces, in terms of the 'twisted' geometry of spacetime in much the same way as gravity and the matter that generates gravity can be described in terms of curved spacetime. The theories are incomplete, but they offer hope of a wonderfully simple view of the universe as just quivering twisted spacetime, changing as parts of it untwist or twist further. Eventually such ideas may revolutionize our understanding of physics and reveal the current inhabitants of the particle zoo to be unreal and imperfect inventions of the human mind, only loosely modelling the true and twisted reality. Such a revolution would leave us with an apology to make to those ancient Greeks who insisted that matter was continuous, despite the dominant views of Democritus, who claimed it was made of little particles and so gave birth to the modern science of particle physics. The entire universe may indeed consist of a continuous twisted 'something' whose tightest twists behave like discrete particles without really being discrete particles at all. If so, then the shopping list for creation considered earlier could be reduced to just one item – spacetime – and the recipe for creation to just one essential process – twisting.

7 Quanta

As we look at the world and try to make sense of its actions, it is natural to try to explain everything in terms of simple things we are familiar with and can understand. The most obvious parts of our world are the land and the sea, and on the land we find hard solid objects such as rocks and stones, while on the sea (and also on rivers and lakes) we find the motion of waves of water. Hard bits of solid and moving waves of water are the two most familiar phenomena of the natural world. In their early efforts to make sense of the world, scientists took these phenomena as reliable models for things in the micro-world. They developed theories of a micro-world composed of tiny hard 'particles' of matter which moved through a sea of 'waves' of radiant energy such as light. There were excellent reasons for supposing that the most fundamental components of Nature had to be either particles or waves, but it was a deceptively simplistic supposition based on the hope, and expectation, that the world of the very small would be similar to our everyday world of the fairly big. Yet the world of the very small, of particles and light, is very different from our own in many puzzling ways. The branch of physics that encompasses these puzzles, and gives us our best view of what the micro-world is really like, is known as quantum mechanics.

The story of quantum mechanics begins with supposed waves of light, which turn out to have a particulate nature as well; it moves on to supposed hard particles, which turn out to behave like waves in important respects; and then develops into a unified view of a universe in which there are no waves and no particles, but which is founded on a mysterious wave-particle duality at the heart of everything. The consequences of taking such a dual and unified view of things are startling, bewildering and extremely useful.

Let's begin by looking at light, and other forms of the type of energy known as electromagnetic radiation. The light energy that floods from the sun, or from the light bulb above your head, is just the visible part of a broad 'spectrum' of what are known as 'electromagnetic radiations', which also include gamma rays, X-rays, ultraviolet rays, infra-red rays, micro-waves and radiowaves. They are called radiations because they radiate outwards from their source, and electromagnetic radiations because they consist of moving fluctuations of the electromagnetic force field. As electromagnetic radiation impinges on something; in other words, it subjects it to oscillating electromagnetic forces capable of pushing and pulling objects that feel the electric force. Electromagnetic radiation is energy on the move at the fastest speed anything can move – the speed of light.

The difference between the various rays of the electro-magnetic spectrum is simply a matter of the frequency of the fluctuations in the electromagnetic force field associated with them. Gamma rays have the highest frequency fluctuations, followed by X-rays, ultraviolet rays, visible light rays, infra-red rays, microwaves and finally radiowaves, with the lowest frequency.

As it moves, electromagnetic radiation behaves very much as if it consisted of waves, a fact recognized in the terms 'microwaves' and 'radiowaves' used above. It seems to be a travelling oscillation or travelling vibration, and that is really all that any wave is. It also shows the characteristic property of waves known as 'interference': when two waves meet, they add together or combine, so that if two troughs of the waves meet they combine to yield a deeper trough, if two peaks combine they yield a higher peak, if troughs and peaks combine they entirely cancel one another out; while all other combinations yield more complex wave patterns as each wave *interferes* with the other. Such behaviour led to the wave theory of light, which reigned unchallenged until the early years of the twentieth century.

It was Albert Einstein – again! – who provided the most significant challenge to the wave theory of light, and it came in a paper published in 1905, the same year as his theory of special relativity was published. In trying to interpret an experiment performed by the physicist Max Planck (famous for a fundamental numerical constant in Nature known as 'Planck's constant'), Einstein said that light, and other electromagnetic radiations, must come in discrete 'packets', or even 'particles', called photons. He proposed that light of any particular wavelength, that is any particular distance between the peaks of its travelling waves, must consist of photons which all carry a discrete and equal amount of energy. This idea of light consisting of a stream of tiny packets of energy called photons has been fully confirmed by further experiment, but what does it mean? Does it mean that light is not wave-like? No, it means that light is truly *neither* simply a wave nor a particle, but instead behaves in a way that contains elements of both these types of behaviour. Einstein expressed it by saying that a full understanding of the nature of light would involve a *fusion* of the wave and particle descriptions, rather than the abandonment of either. Such a fusion is hard, if not impossible, for us to envisage, since none of the objects we are familiar with in the everyday world behave like that. Nevertheless, countless experiments have revealed that light really can behave at times like a form of wave motion and at times like a stream of discrete particles. Light really *is* that way, and it is just our hard luck that we find it difficult to comprehend.

So light does not really consist of waves, nor of discrete particles, in the sense that we normally use those terms. It consists of something else, some unique phenomenon for which there is no exact parallel in the everyday world. One way of attempting to comprehend this idea of wave-particle duality a little better is to think of a photon as a tiny region of localized vibration of the electromagnetic field, travelling along in a coherent manner so that at times it behaves just like a discrete particle, and at times like the vibrations (i.e. waves) of which it is really composed. Such a view allows a photon to be described as a 'wave-packet', although it still provides only a simplistic analogy for the true situation. Notice that it makes the *field* the more fundamental phenomenon, with the particle, i.e. the photon, being explained as a localized and energetic disturbance of the field. This is the way most physicists prefer to think of particles: as localized disturbances of fundamental fields.

As physicists puzzled over the ability of light, long regarded as consisting of waves, to sometimes behave as a stream of particles, further consternation lay before them in the form of the converse of that paradox. A young French physicist called Louis de Broglie (pronounced 'de Broy') soon suggested, in the early 1920s, that particles such as electrons, protons and so on, might also be part of the conundrum by possessing hitherto unknown wave-like properties. By a very simple mathematical argument, he was able to come up with a 'wavelength' for particles such as electrons, but what was the relevance to the real world of this success on paper? De Broglie presented his idea as part of his doctoral thesis, but when his examiners con-templated it in late 1924 they were apparently not particularly impressed. By 1927, however, his theorizing had been fully confirmed by experiment, and by 1929 he had received a Nobel Prize for it. So the relevance to the real world of his theorizing is that electrons really can behave as waves in a way that seems totally baffling if we insist on viewing them as tiny hard particles.

The wave-like nature of electrons, and other particles, can be observed by performing a very simple experiment using just a source of light, a source of electrons, a screen with two holes or slits in it, and some sort of detector for light or electrons on the other side of the screen (see figure 7.1).

If light is shone upon the screen, each tiny hole in the screen behaves like a new source of light from which light waves emanate, as shown in figure 7.1. These two sets of waves interfere with one another in the manner outlined above, so that the intensity of light arriving at different parts of the detector rises and falls in an 'interference pattern'. The highest intensity light is found where the two sets of waves add together perfectly (interfere 'constructively'), with each set's peaks aligned with the other's and each set's troughs aligned

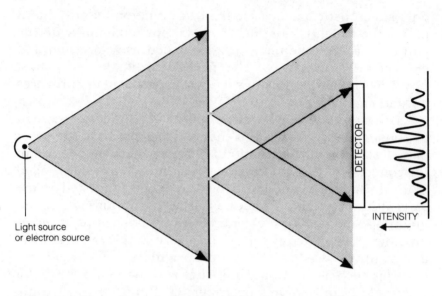

Figure 7.1 Photons and electrons both show wave-like behaviour. See text for details.

with the other's. Dark areas are found where the two sets of waves exactly cancel one another out (interfere 'destructively'); and regions of intermediate light intensity are found where the interference falls between the two extremes of perfect constructive and perfect destructive interference. The occurrence of such an interference pattern is a prime tell-tale sign that a wave-like phenomenon is present.

Now, suppose the light source is replaced by a source of electrons. If electrons were truly tiny hard particles we would expect each one either to pass through one of the holes or to bounce back from the screen. As time passed, a pattern of 'intensity of electron arrival' could be built up on the detector, but we would certainly not expect it to look like an interference pattern. Each electron passing through a hole would arrive at a precise point on the second screen with no prospect of interference from other electrons (other than perhaps collisions which would change their trajectory). The surprising thing that does happen, however, is that an interference pattern *is* found. A chart plotting the number of electrons that arrive at each point on the detector over a period of time looks exactly like an interference pattern. Indeed it *is* an interference pattern, because the electrons show the same puzzling wave-particle duality as photons. Yet more surprising, this interference pattern builds up even when individual electrons are fired from the source *one at a time* – which, if you think about it for a while, means that each individual electron, or something associated with each electron, must somehow go through both holes at the same time!

How should these puzzling results be interpreted? They certainly tell us that electrons do in some way behave like waves, thus abolishing the naive notion that they can be accurately described simply as tiny hard particles. As for what exactly the wave-component of the electron represents, that is the focus of a debate which has still not been satisfactorily settled. The standard, 'establishment' interpretation goes like this. What moves from the electron source and through the screen, going through both holes at the same time to generate an interference pattern, can be regarded as a *'probability wave'* whose intensity at any point is related to the probability of an electron being found at any particular place and time. Individual electrons somehow adhere to the rule of this probability wave, appearing as tiny particles at various points on the detector in the numbers required to make the pattern of electron arrival look just like the interference pattern produced by the arrival of a conventional wave. Precisely how the probability wave controls the behaviour of the individual electrons, or how the individual electrons 'collapse' out of the probability wave pattern, is a complete mystery. This is by no means a fully satisfactory nor fully accepted interpretation. The problem of interpreting the experiment remains, but, whatever such problems, the facts of the experiment cannot be disputed. In a real and thoroughly tested way electrons, and all other supposed 'particles', really do behave in some important respects like waves. There is a true wave-particle duality at the heart of matter, making the individual concepts of waves or particles inadequate to describe the photons, electrons, and other inhabitants of our bizarre micro-world.

What I have presented here is a brief descriptive, qualitative and very general account of the wave-particle duality at the heart of everything. A more rigorously quantitative and detailed account would need to be written largely in the language of mathematics. This is not the place to explore the mathematical details of quantum mechanics, but suffice to say that the general ideas and phenomena described above can indeed be described in a very precise and beautiful quantitative manner using the terse language of mathematics. When that is done, a very significant new feature of the universe emerges. It turns out that it is impossible to pin down events in the micro-world completely. It is impossible, in other words, to describe exactly where everything is and what it is doing; and this is impossible not because of any experimental inadequacy on our part, but *because such determined precision is not a true part of the nature of things.* At the heart of the micro-world we find a deep uncertainty which can never be removed.

This uncertainty is described by 'Heisenberg's uncertainty principle', named after Werner Heisenberg, the German theoretical physicist who discovered it within the mathematical equations of quantum mechanics in 1926. Heisenberg's uncertainty principle can be stated in more than one way. It can be stated by saying that the location and momentum of any object (an electron, photon, proton etc. . . .) can never both be precisely determined simultaneously; or by saying that the energy of a phenomenon and the time the phenomenon lasts for are always associated with a certain degree of uncertainty. Regardless of how the uncertainty principle is stated, it is vital to emphasize that it is not simply describing some deficiency of our ability to *measure* what occurs in the micro-world. Instead, it is believed to reflect a real uncertainty or 'fuzziness' of the micro-world itself. We cannot know the precise position and momentum of an electron, for example, because an electron never actually has a precise position and momentum.

We must abandon the view of the micro-world as composed of tiny particles and waves moving about at definite speeds with definite energies and interacting with one another in a totally fated, deterministic fashion. Instead we must accept that there is an inherent uncertainty dominating events in the realm of the very small, and that the only descriptions we are ever going to get of these events must be probabilistic ones. We can say, in other words, what the probability of a particle doing any particular thing is, but can never pin its behaviour down with 100 per cent certainty, because the particle itself is never fully pinned down into doing a certain thing at a certain place.

This all sounds rather confusing, and it is. When quantum mechanics starts to confuse you then you know you are beginning to understand it! It confuses even the best physicists working at the frontiers of the field, and even they do not properly know what it means. The existence of the inherent uncertainty revealed by quantum mechanics must be accepted, however, because its effects are all around us.

Among its most dominant effects are the fundamental forces themselves, because without the uncertainty principle the particles which are believed to be responsible for these forces would not exist. Earlier (on page 43) we saw that modern physics regards all forces as due to the *exchange* of force-carrying particles between the objects that feel the forces. So if we consider two electrons near to one another, for example, they will be repelled from one another by the exchange of photons of electromagnetic energy which serve as the messenger particles of the electromagnetic force. There is something rather special about these force-carrying photons, however, compared with the photons of light that are allowing you to read this page. The force-carrying photons are known as 'virtual photons' because they can exist only for a certain time determined rigorously by the uncertainty principle.

To learn about this we must focus on one of our pair of interacting electrons, and consider its energy. We might be tempted to say that the electron must possess a certain amount of energy, depending on how fast it is moving and what its surroundings are, but then we remember that the uncertainty principle tells us that the electron's energy is uncertain to a precisely determined degree. Electrons can lose energy by emitting photons, or can gain energy by absorbing photons, and they are completely free to do so at random provided the changes in energy are no greater than the inherent uncertainty in the energy of the electron overall. So all of the time electrons are emitting photons and re-absorbing them, thanks to the freedom allowed by the uncertainty principle. Such photons are referred to as 'virtual photons', to distinguish them from the free photons that we see as light, for example, which are released when particles such as electrons within an atom actually undergo permanent loss of the energy concerned. The virtual photons that are allowed to be released and then re-absorbed thanks to the uncertainty principle are the very ones responsible for the electromagnetic force. Without the uncertainty principle the energy of any electron would be absolutely fixed at any time, so the electron would not be able to release the photons required to carry the electromagnetic force.

What holds for the carriers of the electromagnetic force also holds for the gluons, gravitons and W and Z particles that carry the other fundamental forces. These particles are created and destroyed thanks to and within the limits of the uncertainty principle. If the micro-world were fully deterministic and associated with no uncertainty, the force-carrying particles could not be created, so without the uncertainty at the heart of the micro-world there would be no fundamental forces. Let nobody tell you, as some may try to, that quantum mechanics is of no relevance to the everyday world. Without quantum mechanical effects there would be no gravity, no electro-magnetism, no strong and weak nuclear forces, no chemistry, no biology and no you.

Is determinism dead?

Our lives are embedded within a swirl of other things and events which seem to jolt and jostle us this way and that. The events which affect us – the actions of others, the state of health of our bodies, the weather or whatever – appear very complicated and hard to predict or control. Despite that, we intuitively feel that we do have some ability to influence these events, to take decisions that will perhaps alter some small aspects of the surrounding swirl to send them down paths closer to our liking.

Our apparent understanding of this seemingly natural state of affairs received a severe blow when the science of physics truly began to flourish during the past few centuries. The universe then appeared to consist of tiny hard particles and waves of radiant energy which moved and interacted according to precisely determined laws. All change around and within us, from the orbit of the planets to the whirling of electrons within atoms, was believed to proceed in a completely *determined* fashion. The view arose that if one could know the position and state of motion of every particle in the universe then one could predict all future events with infallible accuracy. Scientific determinism rose in triumph from the swamp of primitive intuition, and suggested that there was no such thing as chance, and presumably no such thing as free will – nothing but a clockwork universe slowly unwinding along its fated path.

Of course, it was never quite as simple as that. Many, even most, phenomena around us appear so complex that it is hard to accept that their development is wholly determined by prior conditions and easier to consider it as somehow random or 'chaotic'. One of the lessons of the emerging science of 'chaos', however, is that what we call chaotic behaviour truly does possess an underlying determinism (although the form of determinism described in the next few paragraphs rather than the preceding one), even though we find it impossible to predict what determined paths so-called chaotic systems will flow along. The science of complexity and chaos is outside the scope of this book, but I recommend the texts on this subject by James Gleick and Ian Stewart, listed in the bibliography at the end of the book. The essential message of chaos theory is that seemingly random and chaotic behaviour within seemingly complex systems may in fact be governed by very simple deterministic processes which are simply highly sensitive to slight changes in initial conditions. It wasn't the science of chaos that led to the downfall of determinism; if anything, its insights could be used to reinforce a belief in determinism underlying even the most complex of events. The threat to determinism came from quantum mechanics.

Totalitarian determinism, whether predictable or unpredictable, had a good reign, but quantum mechanics has knocked it from its throne and left us puzzling about what should be put up in its place. The downfall of determinism, of course, lies in the uncertainty principle. This central tenet of quantum mechanics tells us that the position and motion of particles of matter *is not* precisely determined. It tells us that there is a true uncertainty about such things which must always leave some uncertainty about the paths down which future events will flow. Determinism is not completely overthrown by quantum mechanics, however, for it retains honourable status in the new form of 'probabilistic determinism'. This means that, while the precise course of future events may not be determined, the *probability* of particular outcomes following particular situations is very much precisely determined.

Suppose we are interested in the behaviour of an electron, for example. Classical determinism would tell us that, given enough information about its state of motion and its environment, we should be able to say with utter certainty 'the electron will now do this rather than that'. Quantum mechanics abolishes such certainty, but replaces it with complete certainty about the *probability* of the electron doing this or that. It might tell us, for example, that the probability of the electron doing this is 70 per cent, and the probability of it doing that is 30 per cent. This would not be much help to us in predicting the actions of any one individual electron, or even of a few electrons; but given a very large number of similar electrons, billions for example, we could predict with incredible accuracy that 70 per cent of them would eventually do this while the remaining 30 per cent dutifully did that. Unfortunately we could not predict in advance which electrons were destined to do this and which to do that.

So is determinism dead, or what? If the favoured interpretation of quantum mechanics is correct, then determinism is certainly dead in the strong total sense in which it was once used. The behaviour of individual particles is not precisely fixed and so their fate cannot be precisely determined in advance. Determinism is very much alive and kicking, however, in the form of an 'effective' or 'everyday' practical determinism up in the relatively large-scale world that we inhabit. The reason for the survival of determinism in this altered form is essentially that most events we perceive around us are the effects of vast numbers of similar particles being presented with similar situations. For all practical purposes, for example, it is absolutely determined that if we open a flask containing gas at high pressure, the gas will escape and spread throughout the environment. This is because there is a much greater *probability* that the motion of the gas particles will cause them to disperse rather than stay where they are. Essentially, there are many more ways for dispersal to occur than for the gas to stay where it is, so dispersal is what inevitably occurs. So for practical purposes the behaviour of the gas is deterministic, but it is quite wrong to say that total determinism therefore applies to the system. There is a certain tiny probability that the motion of the gas particles could make them do very bizarre things, causing no gas to leak out of the vessel for a while or perhaps even making the gas become more concentrated within tiny high pressure regions within the vessel. It is just that the probability of such things ever happening, considering the large number of particles that would all need to move in the correct manner, is so small that you could keep filling and opening vessels for billions upon billions of years and still have only a miniscule chance of ever seeing such strange things occur.

The behaviour of gases, liquids and solids around you, and the progress of the chemistry within you, appears precisely determined because almost everything you notice as a single effect is in reality the cumulative result of large numbers of interactions at the particle level. So Determinism (with a capital D) is dead, but effective determinism in the everyday world lives on.

Connecting the parts into the whole

There is one major puzzle thrown up by quantum mechanics of which I have made no mention so far, and yet which must be given at least a brief mention. It poses a fundamental challenge to our conventional view of the universe, and especially to our tendency to try to make sense of things by reducing them to their tiniest parts. It suggests an interconnectedness between the parts of the universe, across vast distances of spacetime, which nobody can yet explain.

To grasp the essence of the puzzle, consider two photons of light emitted simultaneously in opposite directions from some common source. The photons rush off at the speed of light, soon to be incredibly far apart and, according to a conventional view of things, completely unconnected. The mathematical treatment of quantum mechanics, however, says that in some way they remain connected, or at least their behaviour remains *correlated*, in a very puzzling manner. It says that the result of measuring the behaviour of one of the photons can *instantaneously* affect the result of measuring the behaviour of the other. The importance of making some *measurement* on one of the pair of correlated photons is that it causes a definite result to 'collapse' out of the probability wave associated with that photon, although which result is found is not fixed until it actually occurs. The crucial point is that the result found for one of the photons instantly determines what result must be found for the other one, because the results of the two photons are correlated in a precise mathematical way. This baffling effect has been confirmed experimentally, and nobody really knows how to explain and interpret it. It suggests that even if the two photons were allowed to travel to opposite sides of the galaxy they would remain in some way intimately correlated in such a way that what happened to one of them could instantly fix the state of the other one. The full description of this effect and the experiments that demonstrate it are subtle and cannot be explored here (you will find more detailed accounts, probably indexed under 'non-locality' in many of the physics books listed in the bibliography). Its important message, however, can be readily conveyed and understood: quantum mechanics reveals a baffling connectedness between seemingly distinct parts of the universe, which should make us beware of the habit of analysing things and events in terms of their tiny parts while often losing view of the more complex and integrated whole.

It is appropriate to conclude this chapter with a strong warning that the true meaning of the results of quantum mechanics is the subject of considerable debate. I have mentioned this already, but it deserves to be reinforced. Many physicists dispute the conventional interpretation of quantum mechanics outlined above. Some believe that our theory of quantum mechanics is simply incomplete, and that when it is complete many of the seeming paradoxes and perplexities will melt away, especially those concerning wave-particle duality, the true meaning of the wave-like aspect of things that we are used to regarding as particles, and at least some of the probabilistic aspects of the theory as interpreted at present. Many of the physicists who first created the theory of quantum mechanics were unhappy about the interpretation of the theory that eventually became dominant. Albert Einstein, the greatest physicist of our times, and possibly of any other times, resisted the uncertain and probabilistic interpretation of quantum mechanics until his dying day. 'God', he announced in one famous phrase, 'does not play dice.' Many modern (lesser?) physicists will point to a stream of results that can be used to counter this argument, but until the debate within the physics community is settled to the satisfaction of all it would be wise to bear Einstein's scepticism in mind. It is because the debate is not yet settled that I have merely mentioned some of the more baffling results of quantum mechanics, without entering into any lengthy discussion of what they might truly mean. Quantum mechanics is an astonishingly successful theory of physics, there is no doubt about that. It allows the activity of the universe to the predicted and explained better than has ever been possible before; but the standard *interpretation* of exactly what it means about the universe remains insecure, and the theory itself may still be incomplete in several important respects.

8   Creation

Each of us was created in the union of a sperm with an egg, to develop, be born, grow and then live for a while until we gradually deteriorate and die. We have a beginning, a brief existence, and then an end; and we find that most other things around us have a beginning, a period of existence, and then an end. It is natural, then, for us to speculate about the beginning of everything and the end of everything – to ask questions about the origin and the fate of the entire universe. What does science have to say about such questions, the biggest questions of all?

The great value of the scientific method as a means of investigation is that it allows us to predict with considerable accuracy the course of events that are not happening here and now and which we may be unable to experience directly. Normally, of course, this involves predicting the course of future events, since future events are the ones we wish to influence or exploit. It is also possible, however, to examine the present-day world and 'predict backwards', or 'extrapolate' back to find out what things were probably like in the past.

Observing the stars and galaxies that surround us reveals one major fact – they are all rushing away from one another very quickly indeed. The obvious conclusion, as we extrapolate backwards in time, is that the stars and galaxies must have been closer together in the past, and will be found ever closer the further back we extrapolate. It is simple logic to realize that continuing the extrapolation will eventually yield a time at which all of the stuff of the universe was concentrated into one tiny volume at one time and place. This time and place is the instant that has been christened 'the big bang'. The inevitable conclusion we can draw from the current expansion of the universe is that at one time the universe was in an incredibly dense state which then burst outwards to make the vast universe we see now. Of course, since nobody was around to witness the big bang, it remains merely a theoretical description of our universe's earliest days. The big bang theory, however, is by far the dominant account of how the universe arose and developed, although there is intense debate and speculation about the precise processes that took place as the universe developed from its earliest state. In fact, many rival theories of the big bang exist, and some resist using the term 'big bang' altogether, but all describe a universe that grew from an initial tiny and incredibly dense phase into the massive expanding universe we live in now.

As the universe expanded so it also cooled, from an unbelievably hot and energetic swirl of sub-atomic particles into the atoms then stars and planets of here and now. The simpler atoms, largely hydrogen and helium, were created after the big bang and before any stars had formed. Other types of atom were created later by the fusion of simpler atoms within stars (which are hot, although nowhere near as hot as the universe just after the big bang), or from fusions which occurred during the explosive deaths of some stars as 'supernovae'. The history of our universe according to modern physics involves the big bang, a phase of universal cooling, the coalescing of some parts of the primordial gas into stars and their orbiting planets, and then the continuing expansion of the universe while stars burn and die at the same time as new ones are born.

Some people identify the big bang as the moment of creation, the moment at which all the matter and energy and spacetime of the current universe came into being. Others see it as just one extremity of a repeating process of expansion and contraction which the universe undergoes forever, without beginning or end. The second view declares that the present-day universe will continue to expand for a while (a 'while' being very many billions of years), until the mutual gravitational attraction of all the matter in the universe causes the expansion to slow, then stop, then gradually reverse. Everything would then rush inwards at accelerating pace until, after many more billions of years, a 'big crunch' would occur, squeezing all matter and energy and spacetime together for an instant until another big bang sends it rushing outwards again to make a new generation of stars, planets, authors, readers and cosmologists to ponder the nature of it all. There is a pleasing symmetry about the bang, crunch, bang, crunch . . . scenario which certainly makes it very appealing to me; but such matters will be decided by numbers rather than aesthetic appeal. Physicists do not yet know whether there is enough matter in the universe to make it collapse back on itself towards a big crunch, or whether it will continue to expand forever. So the ultimate fate of the universe is uncertain, we must simply wait for a more definitive answer, or perhaps just wait and see.

If the bang, crunch scenario is correct, then it may make little sense to consider the 'origin' of the universe since it may never have had one, it may just *be* and may always have been. Physicists do like to consider the origin of everything, however, since it provides the ultimate test for their theories. 'Creation Cosmology' is a thriving science with many different detailed models available to describe how everything first came into being, if indeed it did. The matter is far from settled, but one of the most startling preliminary conclusions of this work deserves consideration: the insights of quantum mechanics make it respectable to talk of the 'physical feasibility' of our universe arising spontaneously, driven only by phenomena we are already aware of.

The secret lies in the uncertainty principle of quantum mechanics. In one of its forms this principle states that anything at all can happen, anything whatsoever can be created, provided its energy multiplied by the time it lasts for is less than a tiny quantity known as 'Planck's constant'. This is the relation that allows the virtual particles discussed in chapter 7 to arise and transmit the fundamental forces.

Now the universe has clearly lasted a very long time, and it appears to contain an enormous quantity of energy, but there is a surprise awaiting us if we contemplate that energy more closely. It turns out that some of the energy, largely the energy locked up within the mass of matter, must be assigned a positive value when it is treated mathematically; but the gravitational energy associated with the position of the stars and galaxies in space must be assigned a negative value. There is a strong suspicion that both types of energy are present to equal extents, and so will cancel one another out overall! If you are puzzled as to how that can be, consider a rubber ball which has been stretched in some regions and compressed in others. The ball might be full of changing patterns of stretching and compression, and yet when two such regions meet the compression in one could be cancelled out by the stretching in the other, leaving neither stretching nor compression overall.

So just suppose the energy of the universe is a bit like that, with equal amounts of positive and negative energy which cancel to yield a universe of zero energy overall. According to the uncertainty principle, a phenomenon of zero net energy can arise spontaneously and last for as long as it likes, for the total of zero multiplied by the time it lasts can never exceed the value of Planck's constant, no matter how tiny that value is.

Particles and other forms of energy really do seem to come and go according to the dictat of the uncertainty principle. Such events are known as 'quantum fluctuations', and usually involve phenomena with tiny energies lasting for tiny lengths of time; but if the universe's net energy really is zero, then it may simply be the biggest quantum fluctuation of all – a massive outpouring of activity from a cold cradle of empty nothing.

Of course there is a problem with all this, or at least there is for anyone tempted, as many physicists are, to describe it as an *explanation*, rather than a description, of creation. The problem is that it all presupposes the existence of something able to undergo the 'fluctuation' that supposedly gave rise to our universe. The quantum fluctuations that occur all the time and that are well characterized are not fluctuations of pure nothingness, in the strictest sense of the word, but are fluctuations of the vacuum of spacetime, which is, to a physicist, something very different from pure nothingness. To speculate about the origin of the universe as a fluctuation of sheer nothingness merely raises further questions about what we actually mean by 'nothingness' in such a context. What gave this 'nothingness' its ability to fluctuate? Can the concept of a sheer nothingness embodying such 'abilities' be sustained at all, or does the possession of the ability to undergo quantum fluctuation forbid us from calling it nothingness?

Our universe may have arisen as some sort of quantum fluctuation, or it may simply vibrate endlessly from bang to crunch and bang again; but, whatever the true answer, I feel it will remain an answer unlikely to satisfy most of us when we contemplate the origin of the universe or its possible lack of any origin at all. I personally feel that even if the quantum fluctuation theory of the origin of the universe we see around us is correct, the mystery of ultimate creation, if there ever was an ultimate creation, will remain just that – a mystery. The mystery will merely have been moved back one further step to the point at which our comprehension fails. I believe that a mathematical *description* of the origin of matter and energy from nothing is not the same as an *explanation* for that process. That is a personal viewpoint based on the current state of creation cosmology, and I am well aware that many physicists contemptuously dismiss the idea that their successful descriptions of events cannot be regarded as explanations for the events. Delve into some of the books listed in the bibliography, and the books listed in their bibliographies, if you want to try to make up your own mind.

9 Atoms

We live on a world made of atoms, and as parts of that world we are made of atoms ourselves. The atoms are often combined into larger particles called molecules, or altered slightly into particles called ions, but all the variety and complexity of the things of our world is built from the 'building blocks' we call atoms. Chemistry is the name we give to the changes that take place when atoms and molecules and ions interact with one another. So atoms are the fundamental particles of chemistry; but they are not 'fundamental particles' in the true sense, since atoms are themselves composed of varied numbers of three 'sub-atomic' particles, the protons, neutrons and electrons. To understand all chemistry we need delve no deeper into matter than the level of protons, neutrons and electrons, but of course it is possible to dig deeper, not into electrons, but into protons and neutrons, which are each composed of three quarks.

So protons, neutrons and electrons are the stuff of chemistry, the matter that matters in chemical reactions, since they are the building blocks of the atoms that are the building blocks of all chemicals. As chemists investigate the central role of atoms in the chemical world, they must survey a view that extends both inwards and outwards from the atom. They must look inwards to discover the inner nature of atoms, which holds them together and makes them work; and they must look outwards to examine what happens when atoms bump into one another and so 'react' to form new chemicals. All chemistry is encompassed by that view.

We shall look inwards first, to examine protons, neutrons

and electrons to try to understand what they are and how they behave.

Protons have a mass of almost exactly 1 atomic mass unit. In more familiar units this is 1.67×10^{-27} kilograms, which is a mathematician's shorthand way of representing 0.00000000000000000000000000167 kilograms. So compared with the sort of objects we are familiar with, a proton has an incredibly small mass. It is also incredibly small. The diameter of a proton is 1×10^{-15} metres, so it is very small and very light. The mass of a neutron is also very close to 1 atomic mass unit, and it is roughly the same size as a proton as well. There are small differences between the masses and sizes of protons and neutrons, but too small for us to have to bother about. Although protons and neutrons are tiny compared with us, they are very large compared with electrons. The mass of an electron is 9.1083×10^{-31} kilograms, which in more meaningful terms is 0.000545 times the mass of a proton. This means that the combined mass of 1833 electrons is equal to the mass of just one proton. Electrons contain so little matter that they are hardly there at all, yet we shall see that they are responsible for all the richness and diversity of the chemical world.

The really crucial difference between protons, neutrons and electrons – the difference which lies at the heart of all chemical change – concerns the type of electric charge they carry. Protons carry a positive electric charge of +1, neutrons carry no overall charge (they are electrically 'neutral'), while electrons carry a negative electric charge of −1. So protons and electrons are the electrically charged particles within atoms, and remember that objects with opposite electrical charges, such as protons and electrons, will be drawn towards one another by the electromagnetic force; while objects with the same electrical charge, such as protons interacting with protons or electrons interacting with electrons, will be repelled from one another by the electromagnetic force. These forces of electrical attraction and repulsion involving protons and electrons are the forces that bring about all the changes we call chemistry. They push and pull at the protons and electrons of atoms and so manoeuvre them into new arrangements and combinations as chemical reactions proceed. All chemistry can be reduced to a frantic electric dance of whirling electrons and protons; and the electrons are the dancers which move the most as they are pushed and pulled from place to place like the most sought-after partners in a dance hall. The story of chemistry is essentially a story of electron rearrangement.

So atoms are built out of protons, neutrons and electrons, and everthing else is built out of atoms; but how many types of atoms are there – just one, tens, hundreds, millions? In fact 92 different types of atom occur naturally on earth, so the hierarchy of chemical complexity begins with the three sub-atomic particles, which combine to form 92 types of atom, which combine to form the almost limitless variety of chemicals around us and within us. Chemicals which contain just one type of atom are known as 'elements', and obviously there must be 92 naturally occurring elements since there are 92 types of atom. Chemicals which contain different types of atoms combined together are called 'compounds', and there is an uncountably large number of compounds on earth, and a virtual infinity of possible compounds which could be created by allowing atoms to react in different ways and combinations.

The 92 elements, and therefore 92 types of atoms, of the world are listed in 'the periodic table of the elements' (see figure 9.1). The table begins at the top left, with the smallest and simplest type of atom, hydrogen (symbolized by H), and moves through steadily larger and more complex atoms as we read along each horizontal row from left to right, and then down to the one below it, and so on, except where directed by an arrow to jump to a new location. So after hydrogen, the next largest type of atom is helium (He), followed by lithium (Li), beryllium (Be), boron (B), carbon (C), and so on all the way to uranium (U), which is element number 92 and consists of the largest and most complex of the naturally occurring atoms of the earth. (A few larger unnatural atoms have been created artificially in the laboratory).

We must explore the structure of atoms in more detail, and consider the differences between different types. The best place to start is with the simplest type of atom, the hydrogen atom.

A hydrogen atom is a very simple thing indeed. It is a proton

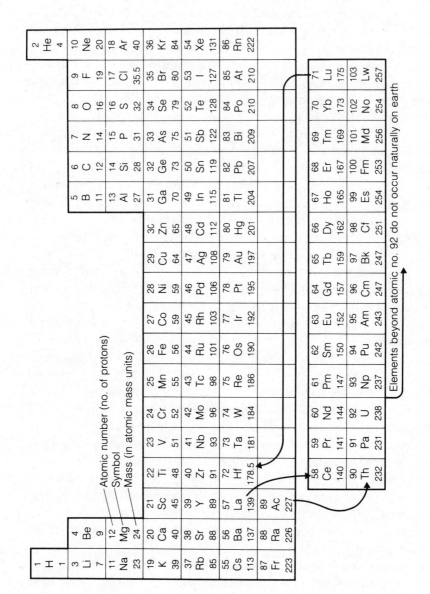

Figure 9.1 The periodic table of the elements.

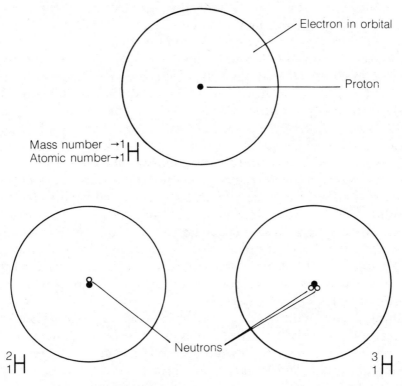

Figure 9.2 The isotopes of hydrogen.

surrounded by an electron (see the top atom of figure 9.2). Looking at this picture of a hydrogen atom presents us with a puzzle: why is the atom so big? We can see the proton at the centre of the atom, but the electron, despite being tiny compared to the proton, appears to occupy a much larger volume of space. Why is the electron not simply nestling up against the proton? After all, it is attracted towards the proton by the electromagnetic force. The answer is that the electron possesses some *energy*, sufficient to keep it from falling onto the proton. The traditional way of thinking about such an 'energetic' electron was to say that the electron must be moving. It must be whirling around the proton a bit like the earth in orbit around the sun. This provides a simple way of explaining why a hydrogen atom can appear so big, despite

71

the smallness of its constituents – we are looking at the size of a mini 'solar system' which is largely empty space.

Sadly, this is a very simplistic and totally misleading picture. Modern chemistry, founded on the principles of quantum mechanics, tells us to regard the electron as a wave or vibration of either 'electron-ness' or of 'probability of finding an electron' occupying the whole of the 'orbital' shown in figure 9.2, and in fact extending to some extent outside of it. An electron's orbital is just a volume of space in which the electron is likely to be found, and the boundary of the orbital is drawn to give a roughly 90 per cent probability of finding the electron somewhere within it. So the probability of finding the electron outside of the boundary is 10 per cent overall, and steadily diminishes the further out you go. So quantum mechanics tells us either to abandon the idea of the electron as a hard little bit of matter, or, if we insist on retaining that idea, to realize that the electron must move about erratically in a way that means we can never know for sure where the electron is and what it is doing at any moment in time. At best we can say where the electron possibly or even probably may be and what it is possibly or probably doing. We can, in other words, only give a probabilistic, statistical description of the electron's behaviour. So, as we consider electrons and their activities in chemistry, it is best to think of the electron as being somehow 'smeared out' within the orbital it is in, and able to make occasional forays across the boundary of that orbital.

If we were able to shrink down to the dimensions of the chemical micro-world and examine a large number of hydrogen atoms, we would discover something a bit different about some of them. In some, the proton at the heart of the atoms would be bound to a neutron. In others, the proton would be bound to two neutrons (see bottom of figure 9.2). These two variant types of hydrogen atom are very rare; we might find only one or two of them for every 10,000 of the normal type, but they do exist and they are important. They illustrate the general point that not all the atoms of any particular element, such as hydrogen, are identical, because atoms of the same element can have different numbers of neutrons present within them. Variations in the number of neutrons present in the atoms of any element do not affect the atoms' basic chemical characteristics. These characteristics, governing what reactions the atoms can participate in, are determined by the number of protons and electrons atoms contain. Chemistry is all about the interaction between positive and negative electric charge, and since neutrons are electrically neutral they have no real influence on the chemical nature of the atoms that contain them, apart from some slight and subtle effects.

All hydrogen atoms contain only one proton, and any atom containing only one proton must be an atom of hydrogen. The number of protons in an atom determines what type of atom it is. In recognition of this importance the number of protons in an atom is known as its 'atomic number'. So the atomic number of an atom defines what type of atom it is. Since all atoms are electrically neutral overall, they must all contain the same number of electrons as of protons, but the proton number is the more fundamental characteristic. When atoms react they can sometimes lose or gain electrons, but the number of protons they contain never changes during the course of a chemical reaction. The 'mass number' of an atom is its number of protons plus its number of neutrons (see figure 9.2). If we know the atomic number and the mass number of an atom, we can work out exactly what its structure is in terms of the three sub-atomic particles.

So the basic principle of atomic architecture is as follows: all atoms of any one type, of any element in other words, contain the same number of protons and electrons and a variable number of neutrons. The variability in the number of neutrons means that atoms of any type come in several varieties which differ simply in the number of neutrons they contain. These varieties are known as 'isotopes' of the element concerned. So, from the information given above, three isotopes of hydrogen exist in nature – the one with no neutrons (and so with a total mass of 1 atomic mass unit), the one with one neutron (total mass = 2 atomic mass units) and the one with two neutrons (total mass = 3 atomic mass units). Remember that the mass of an atom's electrons is negligible compared to the mass of its protons and neutrons, so in calculating the total mass of an atom we can usually ignore the electrons and simply add the number of protons to the number of neutrons to obtain a mass that equals the atom's mass number.

One more term should be introduced before we look at some more atoms. All of the protons and neutrons of an atom are bound together into a tiny central core known as the 'nucleus' of the atom. This nucleus is always tiny compared to the much larger volume in which the electrons are found, although it carries virtually all of an atom's mass. As a rough guide, if the nucleus of an atom were the size of a full stop on this page, the electron orbitals would surround it for many metres or even tens of metres (depending on which element the atom belonged to) in all directions.

Having been told that hydrogen is the simplest element, each hydrogen atom having just one proton in its nucleus and therefore an atomic number of 1, you should not be surprised to learn that atoms of the next element, as we move from the simplest to the most complex, have two protons in their nuclei and so an atomic number of 2. These are called 'helium' atoms. All helium atoms contain two protons, and therefore two electrons, and between one and four neutrons (usually two).

Looking at a helium atom (see figure 9.3) presents us with a new puzzle. It shows the nucleus of the atom containing two protons bound together, yet we know that these protons should be violently repelled from one another by the electric force which pushes apart all objects carrying electric charges of the same sign. You may recall from chapter 3, however, that this is where the strong nuclear force comes into play in the structure of atoms. Protons, and neutrons, carry 'strong charge', or in other words they feel the strong nuclear force. The strong nuclear force is stronger than the electromagnetic force over short distances, while the electromagnetic force can dominate the strong nuclear force over longer distances.

Figure 9.3 Some atoms and their occupied electron orbitals. Shaded orbitals are 'full', i.e. they contain two electrons; unshaded orbitals contain only one electron. The dumb-bell-shaped orbital of boron contains only one electron, although this is largely obscured by orbital overlap.

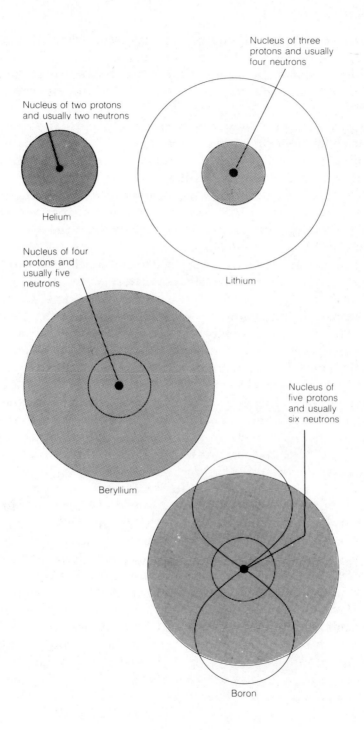

Nucleus of two protons
and usually two neutrons

Helium

Nucleus of three
protons and usually
four neutrons

Lithium

Nucleus of four
protons and
usually five
neutrons

Beryllium

Nucleus of
five protons
and usually
six neutrons

Boron

Within the tight confines of an atomic nucleus the strong nuclear force easily overcomes the electromagnetic force which would otherwise break the nucleus apart. Even so, some large nuclei occasionally do break apart in a process known as nuclear fission.

As we climb the ladder of atomic complexity, the next type of atom we meet has three protons in its nucleus, an atomic number of three, usually four neutrons, and three electrons. Such atoms are called 'lithium' atoms. The diagram of a lithium atom (figure 9.3) introduces a new vital principle of atomic architecture. It shows that two of the atom's electrons are in an inner orbital, much the same size as the orbital that holds the two electrons of a helium atom or the one electron of a hydrogen atom; but that the third electron is in a different, larger orbital. Remember that electron orbitals are simply volumes of space around the nuclei of atoms in which electrons can be found. We will consider more about the underlying logic of such orbitals shortly, but one thing I must say immediately is that it is only possible for two electrons to occupy any one orbital. So two distinct orbitals are required to contain the three electrons of a lithium atom. They are not quite as distinct as might be supposed, however, for the two *overlap* with one another throughout the space occupied by the smaller orbital. The electron in the outer orbital can be found anywhere within that orbital, including the central region which is also occupied by the inner orbital.

After lithium, we move on to 'beryllium', the atom with an atomic number of 4, and therefore comprising a nucleus of four protons and usually five neutrons, all surrounded by four electrons. Remember that there is room in each orbital for two electrons, so the fourth electron of the beryllium atom can fit into an outer orbital similar to the one occupied by the outer electron of a lithium atom. A further principle of atomic architecture can be gleaned from the discussion so far: electrons tend to occupy orbitals which are near to the atomic nucleus in preference to those more distant. Orbitals closer to the nucleus are *lower energy* orbitals, compared to those further out and with a greater volume. Electrons in inner orbitals, in other words, need less energy since their position and motion involves less defiance of the electromagnetic force that would otherwise pull them towards the nucleus. So our new principle of atomic architecture is best stated as: electrons tend to occupy lower energy orbitals in preference to higher energy ones.

We can now summarize the main principles of atomic architecture:

Atoms are composed of protons, neutrons and electrons.

The number of protons in an atom always equals the number of electrons, making all atoms electrically neutral overall.

Atoms of any one type, of any element in other words, all contain the same number of protons and therefore the same number of electrons, although they may contain different numbers of neutrons.

The electrons of atoms occupy volumes of space known as 'orbitals', each orbital containing a maximum of two electrons.

The electrons tend to occupy low energy orbitals in preference to high energy ones.

If we examine the periodic table, we find elements corresponding to all atomic numbers from 1 to 92. There are no gaps in the ladder of natural atomic complexity – there are atoms with every possible atomic number from 1 up to 92. This reflects the fact that complex atoms are made from the combination or 'fusion' of simpler atoms within the interior of stars, or during the explosive deaths of some stars which we know as 'supernovae explosions'. As the universe has developed following its 'big bang' origin, simple atoms, originally just hydrogen atoms, have fused together to yield ever more complex atoms in a stepwise manner that has left no gaps (although of course some atoms are more abundant than others). This history of the universe's atoms is reflected in the fact that, even today, 10 to 20 billion years after the big bang, over 90 per cent of the atoms in the universe are hydrogen atoms. Hydrogen is the fuel for the atom-forging furnaces we call stars, and there is plenty of it left.

There is no point in examining the structure of all the other naturally occurring atoms, since the principles involved should be clear by now; but one further important point about orbitals must be made. If I asked you to draw an iron atom, say of the most common isotope which contains 30 neutrons, you would simply need to draw a nucleus containing 26 protons (since a glance at the periodic table tells you the atomic number of iron, whose symbol is Fe, is 26), 30 neutrons, and surrounded by 26 electrons. Based on what has been said so far you would probably fit the electrons into 13 orbitals of steadily increasing volume and all with the same neat spherical shape as the orbitals we have considered so far. Things are not that simple, however. As we investigate atoms beyond beryllium in the periodic table, we begin to find some electrons in diferently shaped orbitals. Boron, for example, is the element with an atomic number of 5, and its outer electron occupies a twin-lobed or 'dumb-bell' shaped orbital as shown in figure 9.3. Other larger atoms have some of their electrons in more complicated orbitals with four lobes, or even eight lobes, rather than just the two lobes of the outer orbital of boron, with all the lobes projected outwards from the tiny central nucleus. Regardless of their sometimes bizarre shapes, however, the essential fact about electron orbitals is very simple: each orbital is simply a region of space that can be occupied by up to two electrons, and in order to occupy any orbital an electron must possess an appropriate amount of energy, sometimes called the energy level of the orbital.

The energy level of the different orbitals can be presented in diagrams such as figure 9.4. This illustrates a fundamental aspect of the micro-world which we have already met: the energy content of the micro-world varies discontinuously, or in other words is quantized. Entities in the micro-world, such as electrons, seem to be distributed between a series of fixed energy levels, rather than having energies spread freely over a continuous range. An electron can 'jump up' into a higher energy orbital if it absorbs a photon of electromagnetic radiation (such as light) with just the right energy to make

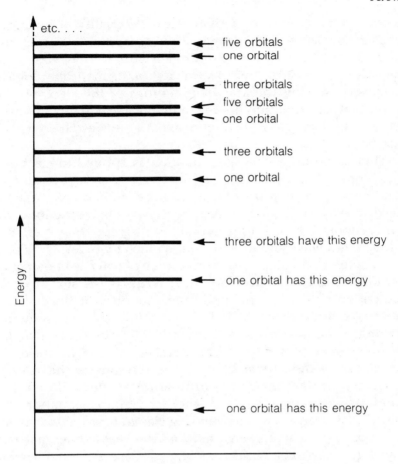

Figure 9.4 The orbitals available for the electrons of atoms are restricted to certain discrete 'quantized' energy levels.

it do so; and an electron in a high energy orbital can 'fall down' into a lower energy one by emitting a photon carrying away the appropriate amount of energy; but in the absence of such absorptions and emissions of electromagnetic radiation, electrons are trapped in the orbitals they occupy.

The modern view of atoms and their electrons emerged from treating electrons as waves, rather than as the hard little particles they had earlier been supposed to be. Strictly speaking, of course, modern physics considers the electron to have properties that are some blend of those of particles and waves, as governed by the wave-particle duality of quantum mechanics which was discussed in chapter 7. It was the German physicist Erwin Schrödinger who, in the 1920s, took the idea of electron waves to its mathematically logical conclusion, taking the known properties of the electron and incorporating them into his celebrated 'wave equation', which allows the behaviour of any wave to be described using numbers.

When Schrödinger's wave equation is applied to electrons surrounding atomic nuclei it yields an infinite number of solutions, corresponding to an infinite number of possible electron waves. If certain seemingly sensible restrictions are imposed on the solutions we should accept, however, the Schrödinger wave equation becomes much more revealing and useful. One particularly interesting type of wave is known as a 'standing wave' or 'stationary wave'. This is the sort of wave you get on a violin string, for example, with different parts of the string vibrating up and down while the wave is not moving along the string at all. Standing waves are essentially just *vibrations* which serve to store energy in whatever is vibrating, so they seem likely to be relevant to the energy stored within the electrons surrounding an atom. If only the standing waves generated by the Schrödinger equation are considered, then a series of standing electron-waves around an atom emerges, whose energy matches the known energy levels found for electrons within an atom. These standing waves are taken to represent the orbitals available for electrons around an atom's nucleus; and the Schrödinger equation also predicts the shape of all the electron orbitals corresponding to various energies. Mathematically speaking, the square of the amplitude of the electron-wave at any location (that is the value of the amplitude multiplied by itself) is taken to indicate the probability of finding the electron at that point at any moment in time. So some rather simple mathematical reasoning reveals a 'shape' for each electron orbital which is really just the position of its '90 per cent probability boundary' as discussed on page 72.

So our picture of the electron orbitals available around atoms is derived from the standing waves of various energies predicted by the Schrödinger wave equation as applied to electrons. These standing waves are not waves in two dimensions, however, like the vibrations of a violin string, but are more like the vibrations within a metal sphere hit with a hammer (although that analogy is not perfect). They are what suggest that an electron around an atom can be considered as a bit like a vibrating cloud of 'electron-ness', rather than as a tiny hard particle rushing around the nucleus. Alternatively, if we insist on retaining the view of electrons as tiny hard particles, then they must be considered to be rushing around erratically within the orbital whose shape is predicted by the Schrödinger wave equation, and with a probability of being in any one place at any one time as predicted by the Schrödinger wave equation.

The Schrödinger wave equation paints the following picture of the electron orbitals around atoms (see figure 9.5). It reveals an atom as surrounded by 'shells' and 'subshells' of orbitals, with room for more orbitals within each shell as we move to higher energies and orbital boundaries further from the nucleus. The shells and subshells are merely collections of orbitals that share a basic mathematical characteristic within the wave equation – they have no physical reality: atomic nuclei are surrounded simply by electrons occupying the volumes of space we call orbitals.

The first shell of orbitals actually contains only one orbital. It has already been said that each orbital can contain up to two electrons, so the first shell has room for two electrons at most. Incidentally, for an orbital to contain two electrons they must have opposite spins, a property of particles discussed on page 42.

The second shell contains a total of four orbitals, and so has room for eight electrons. We can see from figure 9.5, however, that this shell is split up into two subshells of slightly different energies. The lowest energy subshell contains just one orbital, while the other three orbitals of the second shell are of identical but slightly higher energies, and are described as together forming another subshell of the second shell. It is a crucial point that any orbitals belonging to the same subshell correspond to identical energy levels for the electrons within them.

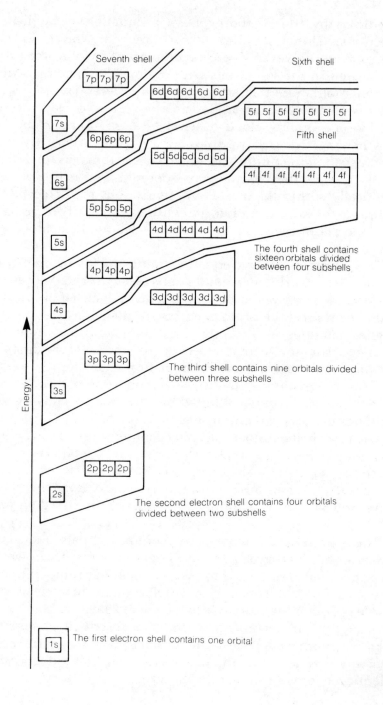

Seventh shell

7p 7p 7p

Sixth shell

6d 6d 6d 6d 6d

7s

5f 5f 5f 5f 5f 5f 5f

6p 6p 6p

Fifth shell

5d 5d 5d 5d 5d

6s

4f 4f 4f 4f 4f 4f 4f

5p 5p 5p

4d 4d 4d 4d 4d

5s

The fourth shell contains sixteen orbitals divided between four subshells

4p 4p 4p

3d 3d 3d 3d 3d

4s

3p 3p 3p

The third shell contains nine orbitals divided between three subshells

3s

2p 2p 2p

2s

The second electron shell contains four orbitals divided between two subshells

Energy

1s   The first electron shell contains one orbital

The third shell contains nine orbitals, and so has room for 18 electrons. It is split into three subshells containing one, three and five orbitals respectively.

The fourth shell contains 16 orbitals, and so has room for 32 electrons. It is split into four subshells, containing one, three, five and seven orbitals respectively.

As we investigate the space around an atom's nucleus, seeking out the orbitals available for electrons with increasingly higher energies, we find the orbitals building up according to a clear pattern, and that pattern continues until we have orbitals available for all 92 electrons of a uranium atom, which is the largest naturally occurring type of atom. The essential feature of the electron orbital pattern is that as we move to higher energies, corresponding to orbitals whose outer boundaries are further from the nucleus, we find room available for increasing numbers of orbitals and therefore increasing numbers of electrons.

When we examine any particular atom in the rather low-energy everyday environment of the earth, we find another pleasing simplicity, already mentioned: electrons tend to occupy the lowest energy orbitals out of all the orbitals available. This state of an atom, in which all its electrons are in their lowest energy orbitals, is known as the atom's 'ground state'. There are many circumstances in which that state can be disturbed by the transfer of energy into the atom, in the form of electromagnetic radiation for example, to make electrons jump up into higher energy orbitals; but the ground state is our basic starting point for a consideration of atoms and their electrons.

The periodic table (figure 9.1), lists all the atoms of the world and allows us to work out how many electrons each contains (since the number of electrons equals the number of protons, which is the 'atomic number' of the atom). So the information in figures 9.1 and 9.5 allows us to identify the ground state

Figure 9.5 The electron orbitals around atoms are assigned to various shells and subshells. (The subshells are known as 's', 'p', 'd' or 'f' subshells for rather technical historical reasons which need not concern us.)

electronic structure of an atom, simply by fitting the required number of electrons into the orbitals shown in figure 9.5, starting with the lowest energy orbital and working upwards until all the electrons are accommodated. A hydrogen atom, for example, contains just one electron, which will be found in the single orbital of the first electron shell – the lowest energy orbital of all. A helium atom, with two electrons, will contain a filled first shell, rather than the half-filled shell of a hydrogen atom. A lithium atom contains three electrons, so while two of them can fit into the single orbital of the first shell, the third will be forced to occupy the lowest energy orbital of the next shell up. A carbon atom contains six electrons, so its lowest energy ground state will have two electrons in the single orbital of the first shell, two in the single orbital of the lower energy subshell of the second shell, and the remaining two in two separate orbitals of the slightly higher energy subshell of the second shell. These two highest energy electrons occupy separate orbitals, rather than pairing off into one orbital, essentially because their negative electrical charge causes them to keep as far apart as possible. This process can be continued to work out the structure of all the atoms of the periodic table (although it is true that a few exceptions do occur, placing electrons, for good reasons, in orbitals where the simple process described above would not predict them to be.)

We have now met all the main principles governing the electronic structure of atoms: electrons occupy the orbitals found around atomic nuclei whose energy and shape are predicted by Schrödinger's wave equation; in their ground state they will occupy the lowest energy orbitals available; and if two or more electrons have orbitals of equal energy available to them they will occupy separate orbitals wherever possible.

If we examine figure 9.5 closely, however, we can find something to trouble us. The figure clearly shows that the orbital referred to as the 4s orbital is of lower energy than the ones called the 3d orbitals. The 3d orbitals are clearly part of the third shell while the 4s one is part of the fourth shell, so why is part of the fourth shell filled before the third shell is complete? The answer we would glean from the table is the true one: the 4s orbital is filled first simply because, in an atom in which all orbitals up to the 3p ones are filled, the 4s orbital is a lower energy orbital that the 3d ones. That leaves the question of why are the 3d orbitals referred to as being in the third shell at all, if they are filled after an orbital referred to as being in the fourth shell? The answer is that the number of shell which an orbital belongs to is a consequence of the mathematics of the wave equation. So the equation which tells us what orbitals are available indicates a mathematical link between all the orbitals referred to as, for example, 'third shell orbitals', and that is essentially why they are called third shell orbitals, even though some of them (the 3d ones) are not filled with electrons until part of the fourth shell is filled. So there is a good mathematical reason for the shell structure outlined in figure 9.5, even though it introduces the complication and seeming paradox that part of the fourth shell becomes occupied before the third shell is complete. The numbering of the shells 'falls out' of the mathematics used to tell us what orbitals are available around atoms; it does not always accurately indicate the relative energies of the orbitals in different shells.

Similar complications can be found higher up the figure, such as the 5p orbitals filling up before the 4f ones. We need not concern ourselves about such complexities when considering the electronic structure of any atom. The *energies* of the orbitals are what matter, rather than the labels we know them by, and the simple rule is that electrons will normally occupy lower energy orbitals in preference to higher energy ones. They will only jump up into higher energy ones if something makes them so jump, such as the arrival of energy in the form of electromagnetic radiation.

That is enough about individual atoms, because although atoms are fundamental and fascinating, what happens to atoms when they collide and participate in chemical reactions is far more important and relevant to the world around us. Most of the substances around us and within us are not free single atoms, but are composed of collections of atoms bonded together. In the next three chapters we must turn our attention to the basic principles that control the interactions of atoms. First, I will use the collisions between atoms to introduce the universally relevant concept of 'entropy'; and then it will be time to turn to the principles behind all of the chemical reactions that make our world and ourselves work.

10 Entropy

Whenever you bask in the heat of the sun, you are being warmed by the phenomenon that makes the universe work. You are taking advantage of the tendency of energy to *disperse*, from places where it is concentrated into places where there is less of it, moving all the time towards a more even distribution overall. The dispersal of energy is the central driving force of all change, and it happens automatically, inevitably, wherever energy has the opportunity to disperse. This chapter explores that dispersal in one very simple situation, to reveal why it happens and encourage you to look for it at the heart of all other situations where change occurs.

Imagine you are holding a long rod of iron, which is a very simple thing in chemical terms because it consists solely of iron atoms on the move. The iron atoms are rushing around, like all particles of matter, colliding with one another to bounce off and rush around some more while participating in further collisions. The iron seems solid and still, but it is full of chaotic motion.

One end of the rod is much hotter than the other, because it has just been pulled from the heart of a furnace, so you are careful to hold the rod by the cool end only; but you know what is going to happen: the heat is going to disperse throughout the rod until some of it reaches the end that you are holding. Everyone knows that heat flows from hot objects to cool ones, or from hot regions of an object into its cooler regions, but we must consider why it does so.

When we say that one end of the iron rod is hotter than the other, all this really means is that the atoms at the hot end are moving faster, or in other words with more kinetic energy, than the atoms at the cool end. The 'heat' of an object is related to how fast its particles are moving. The technical definition of heat tells us that it is a measure of the average kinetic energy of the particles of an object, something which depends on the mass of the particles as well as the speed of their motion. All of the iron atoms in the rod have the same mass, however, so any difference in heat between one end and the other must be entirely due to a difference in the average speed of the atoms in the two ends.

Collisions, however, are constantly occurring between neighbouring atoms throughout the rod, and collisions are great redistributors of energy. To consider what this means think about the extreme case of a fast-moving object – a pool ball, for example – colliding with a stationary one. After the collision you will expect both balls to be moving, and this is indeed always the case apart from one special circumstance in which a full-face blow can stop the initially moving ball and send the initially stationary one moving away. Most collisions are not such special full-face collisions, but are glancing blows which would leave both balls moving. What happens is that the moving ball slows down somewhat, because some of its kinetic energy has been transferred to the initially stationary ball, which speeds up. Energy is neither lost nor gained overall during the collision, but it becomes *inevitably redistributed* towards a more even distribution. Initially one ball had all the kinetic energy, but as a result of the collision that energy has become shared out a bit more evenly. This is the general rule about energy and collisions: when moving objects collide, their energy becomes redistributed in such a way that the objects which initially had the most energy end up with less, the objects which originally had the least energy end up with more, and overall the energy ends up 'shared out' or dispersed more evenly between the colliding objects.

Let's return to the rod of iron, which you are still holding in your hand. Clearly, collisions between the very fast-moving atoms at the hot end of the rod and their slightly slower-moving neighbours are going to cause some heat energy, some motion in other words, to spread along the rod towards the end you are holding in your hand. This happens simply because collisions which move heat energy in that direction are *more likely* than ones which move it in the other direction. To put it another way, there are many more *opportunities* for heat energy to move towards the cool end than there are for it to move in the other direction, and that, essentially, is why the heat disperses throughout the entire length of the rod. This does not mean that collisions in which the direction of energy dispersal takes it towards the hot end never occur – there may well be a few such collisions now and then, but they are much less likely than collisions that disperse heat in the other direction, simply because the atoms at the hot end of the bar are, on average, moving more quickly than those at the cool end.

There you have the essence of the driving force of change that is energy dispersal: *Energy tends to disperse towards a more even distribution simply because there are more opportunities for it to do so than there are for it to become more concentrated in regions that already have a lot of energy.* This might seem a rather long-winded statement of trivial common sense, but it truly describes the driving force of all change in the universe. Everything that happens, from the burning of stars and the earth's cycles of wind and rain to the movement of the muscles that keep you sitting upright and the chemical processes in your brain that are allowing you to think about all this, happens because it is driven forward by the dispersal of energy towards a more even distribution overall.

We have been discussing what is technically known as the second law of thermodynamics, which, despite taking a nominal second place to the well-known first law (the law of conservation of energy) is arguably the most significant physical law of all. In more technical terms, it describes how a phenomenon known as the 'entropy' of the universe inevitably increases. Entropy can be formally defined in various ways, all of which can cause some confusion on a first encounter. In general terms, however, the second law can be simply stated as: 'in any spontaneous change the energy of the universe disperses, overall, towards a more even distribution.' The direction of increasing 'entropy' is the direction of the dispersal of energy. This 'increase in entropy' is why hot things cool down and cool things warm up. It is why the sun can warm you and a dip in the sea can cool and refresh you. It is why ice cubes melt in warm drinks, but do not suddenly form and grow within a hot cup of tea.

Many introductory accounts of entropy describe it as a measure of the 'disorder' present in a system. This allows the second law of thermodynamics to be defined as the inevitable tendency of the universe to become more disordered, overall, as time passes. This rather loose description of the second law can be made more rigorous by considering the ways in which the energy of a system can be distributed within the system. When this is done it again becomes clear that increasing entropy corresponds to the dispersal of energy towards a more even distribution overall.

The universe runs on 'dispersal drive' because, in a universe of chaotically moving particles, there are always more ways for energy to become dispersed throughout the particles than there are for it to become concentrated in small groups of particles. Natural change is guided by the competing probabilities of energy dispersal and energy concentration, with dispersal always winning overall simply because there are many more ways for it to win.

11 Reactions

As we explore the true nature of the world we must work our way up a hierarchy of complexity. A few simple things and phenomena combine to generate a larger set of more complex things and phenomena, and these combine to generate a still larger set of still more complex things and phenomena; and so the hierarchy of interaction and complexity grows until it generates the most varied and complex things we know of – the living organisms whose most complex representatives are human beings. We have examined the first two levels of the hierarchy so far: first, the basic phenomena of physics and the particles created by them; and second, the 92 types of atom of the natural world which are constructed from protons, neutrons and electrons in varying arrays. We will climb towards the top of the pile – ourselves – as we move through chapters 13, 14 and 15; but at the next level up from atoms we find a sudden explosion of apparent variety and complexity: we find the virtually infinite variety of chemical compounds that are created when atoms participate in chemical reactions.

We perform and exploit chemical reactions all of the time. Each morning, for example, I rise from my bed and press a button to ignite the gas that flows from my cooker. The energy of the electrical spark sets off a chemical reaction in which the gas, largely a chemical called methane, reacts with oxygen in the air to generate two new chemicals – carbon dioxide and water – while releasing a lot of heat. I often use the heat to boil an egg, a process which involves chemical reactions within the soft and runny egg to change it into a hard white and yellow mass. Having eaten, I wash myself with a type of chemical we call soap, whose molecules combine with the chemical debris on my body that I want to be rid of, and then I dress and, if I am going out, head for the car. In the car I turn the ignition key to allow the chemical processes within the car battery to generate a spark which ignites another fire. This time it is a fast fire – an explosion – in which molecules within the petrol react with oxygen from the air to generate the waste gases that issue from the exhaust plus the explosive force that pushes at the car's pistons and sets the wheels in motion.

I could continue to the end of the book, describing simply the multitude of chemical reactions which we exploit to live our modern lives. We heat ourselves and generate our electricity using the chemistry of fire, we feed ourselves using the complex chemistry of cooking, we dress ourselves in colourful man-made fabrics thanks to modern industrial chemical processes, we attempt to cure our diseases using the chemistry of drugs, many of which are man-made; and of course within our own bodies our lives are sustained by an incredible complexity of natural chemical reactions.

Chemistry has been called the 'central science', since it occupies the centre ground between physics and biology, and it covers the interesting chemical processes that physics makes possible, and which are required to sustain all living things. It is certainly central to our lives, and in this chapter and the next we shall explore the simple foundations upon which the complexity of chemistry is constructed.

The essential events within all chemical processes are chemical 'reactions'. When chemicals 'react', what they are reacting to is the collisions between the particles they are composed of. The particles that collide and react in chemistry are not just atoms, but also the 'molecules' and 'ions' which can be derived from atoms, and all chemical reactions involve two or more such particles colliding to react by giving rise to something new.

The simplest reaction will involve the simplest atoms, which are the hydrogen atoms that contain one proton and one electron. When hydrogen atoms collide they often simply bounce off one another, but sometimes they react to form a hydrogen molecule, as can be seen in figure 11.1. A hydrogen

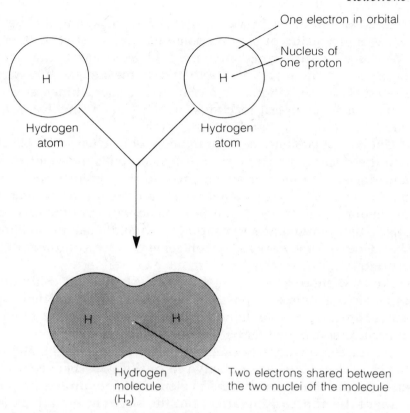

Figure 11.1 The formation of a hydrogen molecule.

molecule is merely a rearranged form of two hydrogen atoms, in which the identity of the individual atoms is lost as they merge into a new single particle. In this new particle the electrons are *shared between* the two protons (between the two nuclei, in other words) rather than each electron surrounding just one of the atoms. The shared electrons occupy 'molecular orbitals' surrounding the two nuclei, rather than atomic orbitals surrounding only one nucleus. In a loose sense the hydrogen molecule can be regarded as an atom with two nuclei.

Whenever atoms combine by sharing electrons we say that a molecule has been formed, regardless of how many atoms are present and how many electrons are shared. So molecules are defined as particles in which two or more atoms are held together by virtue of sharing some electrons between them. We describe such conglomerations of atoms as being held together by chemical 'bonds' between the atoms; but why should chemical bonds form? Why do they sometimes break? What makes chemical reactions, which usually involve both bond-breaking and bond-making, proceed?

Chemical reactions are what happen when chemicals collide and the electromagnetic force pushes and pulls their electrons and nuclei into new arrangements. So the kinetic energy of motion and the electromagnetic force are the initiating agents of chemical change, although our consideration of the second law of thermodynamics in chapter 10 should make us look for the dispersal of energy as the controller of the direction of that change.

To look more closely at the simplest possible reaction, forming the simplest possible molecule, held together by the simplest possible bond, imagine two hydrogen atoms approaching one another on collision course. As they approach, forces of electric attraction and repulsion between the atoms begin to build up. An attractive force develops between the electron of each atom and the nucleus (a single proton in this case) of the approaching atom; but the electrons of each atom repel one another, and the two positively charged nuclei also repel one another. When the collisions between the atoms occur with energies and orientations that allow the repulsive forces to dominate, the atoms bounce apart; but some collisions bring the atoms together in ways that allow the attractive forces to win, because they initiate a complete rearrangement of the electrons which, overall, results in a combined structure *with lower energy* than the separate atomic arrangements. The lower energy structure is the one in which the two electrons are shared between the two nuclei, leaving the atoms joined together by a chemical bond.

So what happens to the energy left over as a result of the atoms settling into their new lower energy molecular arrangement? It cannot disappear into nothing, but must be transferred somewhere else. Some of it may be lost in the form of electromagnetic radiation, given out as electrons fall from high energy orbitals occupied during the chaos of collision to the lower energy orbitals of the final molecular state. Many chemical reactions give out light, such as the light of an explosion, as electrons fall from high energy orbitals which they are temporarily pushed up into during the reaction collision.

Energy lost in the electronic rearrangement of a reaction can also be stored for a while within the products of the reaction, such as a hydrogen molecule, in the form of internal vibrations of the new molecule. Chemical bonds are a bit like springs and the two atoms of the hydrogen molecule can bounce in and out as the bond stretches and compresses. As it stretches, it moves the molecule into a higher energy arrangement because it is stretching against the pull of the attractive forces holding the molecule together; and as it compresses it moves the molecule into another high energy arrangement because it is compressing the nuclei too close to one another, against the force of electric repulsion between them. So a bond that is vibrating in and out stores some energy, just as a spring vibrating in and out holds more energy than one sitting quietly in its uncompressed and unstretched state.

Such energy of bond vibration is soon lost, however, as it becomes dispersed out to the surroundings as a result of the collisions between the new hydrogen molecule and the other particles all around it. Just as a fast-moving molecule slows and a slow-moving one speeds up when the two collide, so a fast vibrating bond will lose some of its energy of vibration as its molecule collides with other molecules which are moving more slowly and whose bonds are vibrating less. Collisions between particles cause all forms of motion to become dispersed towards an even distribution: not just 'straight line' overall motion, but also all of the vibrations and flexions of the bonds and any spinning motions of a molecule overall or some of its parts. Molecules are a bit like tangled balls of springs, with each spring representing a bond. The balls of springs move about and vibrate, rotate and collide, and as they move around and collide both their overall kinetic energies and the energy of all their internal vibrations and rotations tend to become evenly distributed throughout the entire 'balls of springs' population.

So the energy difference between the free atomic state of two hydrogen atoms and the combined molecular state is soon dispersed into the gross and internal motions of all the particles all around. This can leave the new molecule trapped in its new lower energy molecular form – trapped because the energy which could raise it back into the free atomic form has dispersed away into the surroundings. A chemical reaction has taken place because the motion of two atoms brought them together and the electromagnetic force manoeuvred their electrons and nuclei into a new arrangement; but the change has been fixed or stabilized by the dispersal away of the energy lost in the process. The kinetic energy of motion and the electromagnetic force have combined to initiate and complete the reaction, but the reaction has been given direction and permanence by the dispersal of energy – the fundamental guiding force of all change.

Another simple, but slightly more complicated, chemical reaction takes place when water is formed from a mixture of oxygen and hydrogen gases. This is an explosive reaction – one that releases so much energy so quickly that it creates an explosive blast of fast-moving molecules and compressed gases that is used, for example, to propel the US space shuttle into orbit (assisted by the different explosive reactions within the solid booster rockets strapped to the shuttle's sides).

Oxygen gas is composed of oxygen molecules each containing two oxygen atoms (and so symbolized as O_2) which are held together by shared electrons (see figure 11.2). Each oxygen atom contains 8 electrons (and of course 8 protons in its nucleus), so there are 16 electrons in each oxygen molecule. Hydrogen gas is composed of hydrogen molecules (H_2), each containing two hydrogen atoms held together by shared electrons. Each hydrogen atom, however, contains only one electron (and one proton), so there are only two electrons in a hydrogen molecule. The water molecules that are made when hydrogen and oxygen molecules collide and react are each composed of one central oxygen atom bonded to two hydrogen atoms (see figure 11.2), making the chemical 'formula' for water H_2O.

The reaction between hydrogen and oxygen to form water

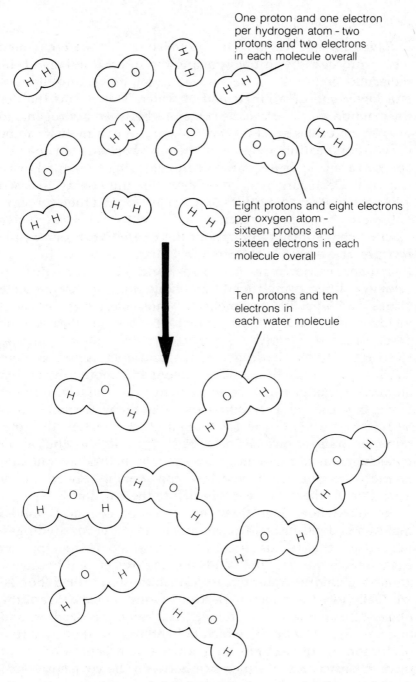

One proton and one electron per hydrogen atom - two protons and two electrons in each molecule overall

Eight protons and eight electrons per oxygen atom - sixteen protons and sixteen electrons in each molecule overall

Ten protons and ten electrons in each water molecule

Figure 11.2 Hydrogen molecules and oxygen molecules combine to form water molecules.

involves a major rearrangement of electrons, a rearrangement which proceeds by initially raising the internal energy of the molecules before it can be allowed to fall down into the new and lower energy arrangement of water. This means that for the reaction to take place the collisions between hydrogen and oxygen molecules must be very violent, something that can be ensured by heating up a few of them by applying a flame or a spark to a small portion of the hydrogen/oxygen mixture. Just a tiny flame or spark will be enough, for the energy released when the first few molecules of water are formed then serves to jolt many more into reacting, leading to a fast explosive reaction that spreads throughout the entire hydrogen/oxygen mixture at a speed that seems instantaneous to us. It is not instantaneous down in the micro-world, of course, and it is actually rather complicated, involving lots of intermediate stages and unstable fragments of molecules, but overall it yields a nice neat rearrangement of electrons that can be described very simply. Each oxygen atom ends up sharing electrons with two hydrogen atoms, and each hydrogen atom sharing electrons with an oxygen atom and another hydrogen atom. The total positive electrical charge (i.e. the total number of protons) carried by the three nuclei in the water molecule is $8+1+1 = 10$, while the total negative charge (i.e. the total number of electrons) is also $8+1+1 = 10$. So the water molecule, like all molecules, is electrically neutral overall, and its electrons and nuclei are in a considerably lower energy arrangement than they were in before the reaction.

We have now met three examples of chemical bonds: the bonds holding hydrogen atoms together in hydrogen molecules, the bonds holding oxygen atoms together in oxygen molecules and the bonds holding oxygen and hydrogen atoms together in water molecules. All these so-called 'bonds' are really just the effect of electrons being *shared between* the nuclei of different atoms, rather than being localized around just one atom. All bonds which hold atoms together by virtue of the sharing of electrons are known as 'covalent bonds', but there is an important difference between the covalent bonds holding oxygen or hydrogen molecules together and the ones holding the water molecule together. In a hydrogen molecule the electrons are shared *equally* between the nuclei of the two hydrogen atoms, since both nuclei carry the same amount of positive charge: $+1$. It is, after all, the positively charged nuclei which attract the negatively charged electrons and so share them between one another. By 'shared equally', I mean that the electron orbital containing the shared electrons is perfectly symmetrical, rather than being biased towards any one nucleus. A similar situation exists in an oxygen molecule: the nucleus of each oxygen atom carries a positive charge of $+8$, so the electrons are shared equally between them.

In a water molecule, however, the electrons which hold the molecule together are shared between an oxygen nucleus with a charge of $+8$ and two hydrogen nuclei each with a charge of $+1$. The electrons are obviously more strongly attracted towards the oxygen nucleus than to the hydrogen nuclei, so the orbitals occupied by the shared electrons are not symmetrical but are distorted in favour of the oxygen nucleus. This means that the molecule carries a slight negative charge around the oxygen atom, since that region of the molecule has a greater share of the shared electrons, while there are regions of slight positive charge around the hydrogen atoms which are slightly 'robbed' of electrons by the oxygen nucleus. Such slight or 'partial' charges are denoted as δ^+ and δ^- charges, to distinguish them from the full positive and negative charges we denote as $+$ and $-$.

Covalent bonds involving the *unequal sharing* of electrons, such as the bonds of a water molecule, are known as 'polar covalent' bonds, since the unequal distribution of electrons causes a polarization of electric charge into a slightly negative (δ^-) 'pole' and a slightly positive (δ^+) pole. Obviously the extent of polarization depends on the difference between the electron-attracting power of the specific nuclei involved. The electron-attracting power of an atomic nucleus when its atom is involved in a covalent bond is known as the 'electronegativity' of the atom.

Electronegativity is one of the central concepts of chemistry, so it deserves further exploration. All chemistry can be viewed as a contest between the nuclei of atoms for the electrons which they are so strongly attracted to. As chemical reactions proceed, the atomic nuclei within the chemicals 'fight it out' to gain the strongest possible hold on the available electrons. In some cases atoms end up sharing electrons equally in covalent bonds; in others they share the electrons unequally in polar covalent bonds; while sometimes electrons are completely won by some atoms and completely lost by other atoms to form another type of bond known as an 'ionic bond', discussed below.

How well any atom is likely to fare in the contest for electrons depends on how strongly its nucleus can pull electrons towards it. That pulling power depends on two factors – the size of the positive charge on the nucleus (in other words, how many protons it contains); and the extent to which the nuclear charge is 'screened', and so its pulling effect reduced, by the repulsive effect of the electrons already surrounding it. The electronegativity of an atom is a quantitative measure of how strongly it can pull electrons towards itself – it is a number, in other words, whose value gives a measure of electron pulling power.

The most electronegative atoms are found towards the top right of the periodic table (see figure 9.1 on p. 70), while the least electronegative (sometimes called the most 'electropositive') are at the bottom left; and in general the further apart any two atoms are in the periodic table the greater will be the difference in their electronegativities. These trends mean that the atoms of elements fairly close together in the periodic table tend to become involved in polar covalent bonds when they are combined into chemical compounds. Since they are close together, their electronegativities will be somewhat similar and so they will share electrons, albeit a bit unequally with the bias towards the most electronegative atom. Atoms of elements that are far apart in the periodic table, however, often participate in the different type of bonds known as ionic bonds. These are formed when one atom is sufficiently more electronegative than another to pull one or more electrons off the other. We shall consider such ionic bonds now, after emphasizing again the central importance of electronegativity in chemistry. An atom's electronegativity indicates its 'ranking' in the grand competition for electrons which lies at the heart of all chemical change. It allows us to make sense of the results of each of the individual contests for electrons that we call chemical reactions, and it allows us to predict the likely results of reactions that we have not yet observed.

As I have said, when some atoms come together and react, the difference in their electronegativities is so great that electrons are completely pulled off one atom and transferred to the other. Reactions like this, which involve the transfer of electrons, create particles with an overall electrical charge called 'ions' which can be held together by 'ionic bonds'. The simple chemical known as sodium chloride, familiar as the 'table salt' we sprinkle on our food, will serve as a good example of an 'ionic compound' held together by such ionic bonds.

Consider a sodium atom and a chlorine atom, shown in very simple form in figure 11.3. When sodium and chlorine react together each sodium atom 'donates' an electron to a chlorine atom, as shown in the figure. This creates a new situation in which the sodium atom has been converted into a particle which is no longer electrically neutral – into an ion, in other words. Its nuclear charge of +11 is now counterbalanced by only 10 electrons rather than the original 11, leaving an overall charge of +1 on the sodium ion (denoted Na^+). The original chlorine atom has also been converted into an ion, called a chloride ion, but this is a negative ion (denoted Cl^-), since one negatively charged electron has been gained. The Na^+ and Cl^- ions are strongly attracted towards one another by the electromagnetic force, so as soon as they are formed they can move together to become 'stuck' to one another by what is known as an ionic bond. This bond is essentially just the force of attraction between the positive and negative ions.

If you could peer down to the level of the ions in a grain of salt you would see an extended three-dimensional network of sodium and chloride ions all held together by ionic bonds in a regular array known as an ionic 'lattice'. There are no molecules in this lattice, since molecules are electrically neutral particles in which two or more atoms are held together by covalent (including polar covalent) bonds, and there are no free atoms, since all atoms are electrically neutral overall.

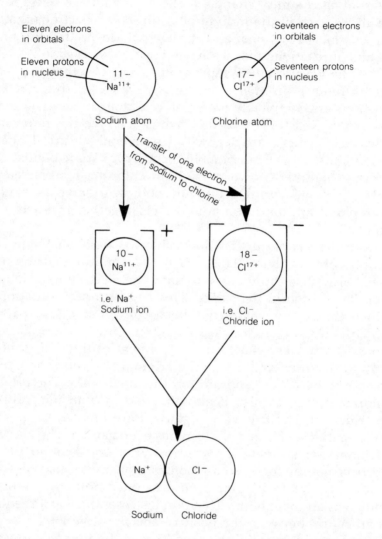

Figure 11.3 The reaction of sodium and chlorine atoms to form sodium chloride, held together by an ionic bond. (Chlorine normally exists as Cl_2 molecules but a free atom has been used here for simplicity. When sodium reacts with CL_2 molecules each sodium atom donates an electron to one chlorine atom overall, so the principles and end results of the reaction are the same.)

Instead there are just ions – the third and final basic type of particle in chemistry – derived from atoms that have lost or gained electrons to be left with an overall electrical charge. The particles of chemistry are atoms, molecules and ions; all of which are themselves made up of the sub-atomic particles protons, neutrons and electrons.

Having been introduced to an ionic bond you may be wondering why it forms, and by now you will probably expect the answer to involve energy and its dispersal. The final state of figure 11.3, with a sodium and a chloride ion nestling against one another, is a lower energy configuration than that at the start of the reaction in which the sodium and chlorine atoms are free and unreacted. The energy released by the formation of the ionically bonded state will normally be dispersed away into the surroundings, leaving the sodium and chlorine trapped in their new ionic form. So reactions which generate ions and ionic bonds occur for the same reasons as reactions which generate molecules and covalent bonds – they occur because the inevitable tendency of energy to disperse makes them do so.

The ions of many ionic compounds carry multiple charges, such as +2, −2, +3 or −3, as a result of losing or gaining more than one electron during their formation. Such multiply charged ions assemble into lattices held together by ionic bonds, just like the sodium and chloride ions considered above, although the precise structure of different ionic lattices differs. If the charges on the positive and negative ions are of equal magnitude, such as +2 and −2, than the ions will again occupy their lattice in a 1:1 proportion. If the magnitudes of the charges on the positive and negative ions differ, then the ions will be present in the proportion that creates an electrically neutral lattice overall, two ions of +1 charge for every one ion of −2 charge, for example.

One further complexity is that many ions are so called 'molecular ions' or 'compound ions', consisting of several atoms that are covalently bonded together, but carrying a positive or negative electrical charge overall. Common examples are ammonium ions (NH_4^+), in which a central nitrogen atom is covalently bonded to four hydrogen atoms and the entire complex carries a single positive charge; and carbonate ions (CO_3^{2-}), consisting of a carbon atom covalently bonded to three oxygen atoms and all with a charge of -2 overall. Such complex ions also assemble into ionic lattices.

We have now met the three main types of strong bonds which hold atoms and ions together to give the objects around us their impression of substance and solidity. These are the pure covalent and polar covalent bonds formed by the sharing of electrons between atoms (often collectively called just covalent bonds, on the understanding that pure covalent bonds only form between identical atoms); and the ionic bonds which hold together ions carrying opposite electrical charges. In all cases, of course, the one ultimate 'binding force' is responsible for binding atoms and ions into larger assemblies: namely, the electromagnetic force which draws opposite charges together (and pushes like charges apart). There are a few other types of bonds to be considered, however, before we have seen the full range of 'glues' available in the world of chemistry. These are the rather distinctive bonds that hold together the atoms of metals, and some very weak bonds that exist *between* atoms and molecules, rather than within them.

The majority of elements, found on the left of the periodic table, are known as metals. The classification of elements into metals, metalloids and non-metals is based on a variety of characteristics. One of the most distinctive of these is that the atoms of metals tend to have only a few outer electrons, and one or more of these outer electrons tend to be able to escape from the atoms rather easily. Within the structure of a piece of metal these escaped outer electrons can wander around from atom to atom, so that the structure of a metal consists essentially of an array of positively charged metal ions surrounded by a 'sea' of mobile electrons. This electron sea within the structure of metals explains why they conduct electricity so readily. An electrical current is just a flow of electrons from one place to another, and the electron sea within metals provides plenty of free electrons which can form such a flow. The electron sea of a copper wire, for example, will flow towards any region of positive charge at one end of the wire and away from a region of negative charge, and therefore a source of replacement electrons, at the other end of the wire. Such flows of electrons through the structure of metals allows the metals to act as electrical conductors within electrical circuits.

The electron sea within a metal also acts as a sort of 'electric glue' holding any piece of metal together. The escaped outer electrons are electrically attracted to the metal ions left behind, so they tend to hold these ions together, and hence hold the structure of any piece of metal together. This phenomenon is known as 'metallic bonding' since it bonds the individual particles of a metal into one cohesive structure.

Covalent, ionic and metallic bonds are strong bonds – bonds, in other words, which can only be broken by a substantial input of energy. There are many much weaker and more subtle chemical bonds, however, which generally form weak attractive forces between distinct atoms and molecules. Despite their relative weakness, in fact often because of that weakness, which allows them to be readily broken and remade, these are some of the most vital bonds of all. We should give them due consideration.

We have seen how ions carrying a full positive charge and ions carrying a full negative charge are drawn together into an ionic bond. Many chemicals carry the *partial* electrical charges associated with polar covalent bonds, and such regions of *partial* charge can serve to draw different molecules together and hold them in a loose complex. Water molecules provide one of the best examples (see figure 11.4). Remember that the hydrogen atoms of a water molecule carry a δ^+ charge, while the oxygen atom carries a δ^- charge, all because the bonds between the oxygen and hydrogen atoms are polar covalent ones. As you can see from figure 11.4, this allows the electric force to pull water molecules into a loosely bonded network in which all of the hydrogen atoms are held close to oxygen atoms, and vice versa. There is a force of attraction, in other words, between neighbouring water molecules, and it is known as a 'hydrogen bond' due to the central role of hydrogen atoms in holding the water molecules together. This attractive force is very weak, compared to full covalent, polar

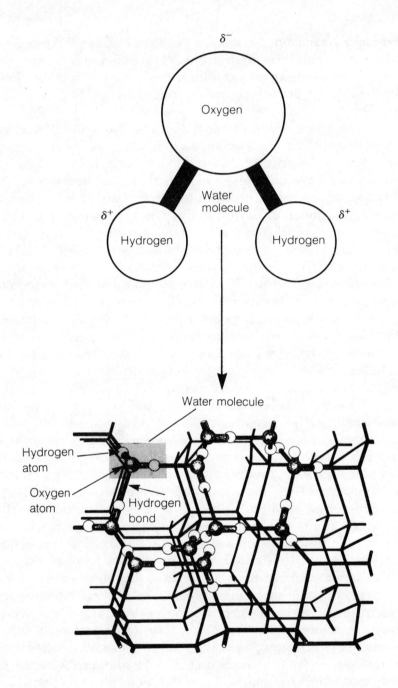

Figure 11.4 Hydrogen bonding in water (see text for details).

covalent or ionic bonds, and so the cage-like structure of figure 11.4 is easily disrupted by the input of some heat energy. It extends throughout large volumes of water only when that water is frozen into ice, but even in a glass of water at room temperature there will be small regions of this cage-like structure, and all of the water molecules experience a weak attractive force from their neighbours even though many may be tumbling over and around one another. This force of attraction has some very significant effects. For example, it makes the boiling temperature of water 100 degrees centigrade, whereas without it water would boil at a much lower temperature since less heat energy would be needed to separate the molecules into gas. Without the effect of these weak intermolecular bonds, life as we know it could never have arisen on earth – all the water within the cells of our bodies, as well as the water of the seas and rivers and lakes, would boil away into gas. So these intermolecular forces, although weak, are very significant.

There are even weaker forces of attraction between all atoms and all molecules, known as Van der Waals forces or Van der Waals bonds. To understand their origin we must appreciate that regions of very slight positive and negative charge constantly appear and disappear on the surface of any chemical. It is as if the random motion of all the electrons continually creates and soon destroys regions where electrons have momentarily become concentrated in one region and depleted elsewhere. When such regions of slight positive charge happen to form opposite regions of slight negative charge on neighbouring molecules, the two regions will be drawn towards one another and will tend to stabilize one another. The stabilization occurs because the slight positve charge on one molecule attracts electrons of the other molecule towards it and so reinforces the other molecule's region of negative charge; while that region will repel electrons from the positively charged region of its partner and so reinforce it. If regions of the same charge happen to arise opposite one another, there is no such stabilizing effect; in fact, each tends to destroy the other.

So there are very weak Van der Waals forces operating

between all neighbouring atoms and molecules which tend to draw the neighbours gently together, and hold them together, unless they are swamped by other more powerful effects.

We have now met all the main bonds or 'binding forces' of chemistry: the full covalent, polar covalent and ionic bonds; and also the weaker bonds that can pull neighbouring atoms and molecules more gently together. Whatever the details, however, it is the electromagnetic force of attraction between positive and negative electrical charge which forms the binding force of all chemical bonds. Chemical reactions are what happen when the particles of chemistry – atoms, molecules and ions – collide to allow the electromagnetic force to push and pull at their electrons, breaking some existing bonds and allowing new ones to form. That is the essence of chemistry, but there is a lot more to be said about some of its complexities and subtleties. We will deal with some such complexities and subtleties in the next chapter, and in the process gain a much better overall view of the nature of chemical reactions.

One vital aspect of chemical reactions can be covered here, however, as we look back on our quick initial survey of chemistry. We have seen how hydrogen, an explosive gas, and oxygen, the gas that sustains fires, can react together to generate water, a liquid used to put out fires. And we have seen how sodium, a metal which bursts into flames on contact with water, and chlorine, a poisonous gas, can react together to generate sodium chloride which we happily sprinkle on our food! These two reactions vividly demonstrate the power of chemistry to transform the characteristics of the chemicals that react together. When chemicals react to adopt a new form, the characteristics of the products are often totally different from those of the starting materials. All that happens during a reaction is that the electrons and nuclei of the products become rearranged in some way. So at the end of a reaction the same types of atoms are present as were present at the start, the same electrons and the same nuclei; but the *arrangement* of these components has changed. Chemistry is always a process of *rearrangement*, regardless of the specific chemical reaction involved; and the great power of chemistry is that mere rearrangement of the bits and pieces of chemicals – their electrons and their nuclei – can utterly transform their characteristics.

12   Equilibrium

To help us explore the essence of chemistry a little more than was done in chapter 11, we need a new type of diagram known as the 'energy profile' diagram of a reaction. A very simple one is shown in figure 12.1a, illustrating in a very approximate and generalized way the energy changes that take place when molecules of nitrogen (N_2) collide with molecules of hydrogen (H_2) to generate molecules of ammonia (NH_3). The stability of Western society is dependent upon this simple little reaction, because the ammonia it generates is needed to make many of the fertilizers which support the intensive agricultural methods which feed us. The importance of the ammonia is that it contains the element nitrogen, vital for the growth of plants.

The reaction which forms ammonia can be summarized by writing a chemical *equation*, which simply shows the 'formulae' of the chemicals involved (i.e. their symbolic representations, such as N_2 etc.) and the proportions in which they react overall. For the formation of ammonia from nitrogen and hydrogen the equation is:

$$N_2 + 3H_2 \rightarrow 2NH_3$$

which can be translated into the sentence 'one molecule of nitrogen (containing two nitrogen atoms) reacts with three molecules of hydrogen (each containing two hydrogen atoms) to generate two molecules of ammonia (each containing one nitrogen atom and three hydrogen atoms).' Stating what happens in equation form is clearly more concise than relating the same information in words, even for this very simple

110

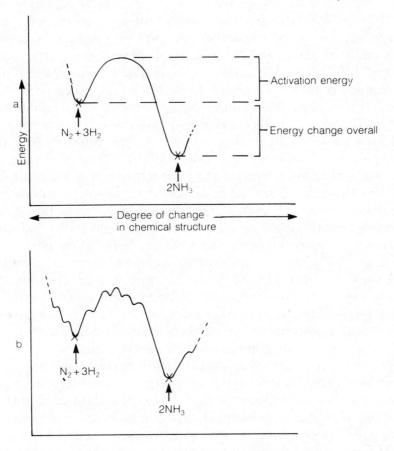

Figure 12.1 Energy profile diagrams of a chemical reaction (see text for details).

reaction. That is why chemists use chemical equations to describe reactions, and with more complicated reactions the translation into words of a one-line equation could run to many lines. It is important to remember, however, that all of the information expressed in a chemical equation could easily be written in plain words instead – there is nothing magical or mystical or particularly difficult about chemical equations, once you get used to them; they are just concise representations of information which could be conveyed with words.

111

Notice that there are two atoms of nitrogen on the left-hand side of the equation, where the starting materials of the reaction are listed, and also two atoms of nitrogen on the right-hand side, where the products are listed. There are also equal numbers of hydrogen atoms on both sides of the equation, six on each side. Such equalities or 'balances' are essential for an equation to be correct, because atoms cannot be created or destroyed or changed into other types of atoms during the course of a chemical reaction. As has been emphasized already, all that happens during a reaction is that the available atoms become *rearranged* as the bonds between them change, due to the rearrangements of the available electrons. Equations with equal numbers of each type of atom on either side are known as 'balanced' equations. Nature balances its equations automatically, since reactions in which no atoms are created, destroyed or transmuted from one type into another are the only ones possible in Nature (although the transmutation of one type of atom into another can occur, but not as a result of a chemical reaction). Humans sometimes find it much more difficult to work out how to balance an equation.

Having summarized the essentials of chemical equations, it is time to consider properly the energy profile diagram of the reaction that forms ammonia. It takes the form of a simple graph, in which the vertical axis corresponds to an energy scale. Suppose we were able to work out exactly how much 'internal' energy was held by an assembly of nitrogen molecules accompanied by three times as many hydrogen molecules at some chosen temperature. We would then know exactly how much potential energy and kinetic energy was stored internally, within the structure of each molecule. All this energy held by the assembly of molecules would add up to some figure, and we could indicate this energy content by putting a cross labelled '$N_2 + 3H_2$' at an appropriate height on our graph. No figures are required on the energy axis, however, if we are merely interested in the relative size of *changes* in energy content, rather than in the precise values of such energy changes. Even if we are interested in precise values, measuring the precise changes in energy during the course of reactions is sufficient, rather than attempting to measure the actual energy content of the chemicals involved. From an experimental point of view, measuring such changes in energy is much easier than measuring actual energy contents.

The horizontal axis of our graph is labelled 'degree of change in chemical structure'. This means that movement along this axis, in either direction, corresponds to bringing about some change in the structures of the nitrogen or hydrogen, or both. This is a very general and approximate idea which again requires no figures on the axis if we are simply interested in a general way in how the energy level of the chemicals changes as their normal electron arrangements are altered. The curve drawn in the diagram shows that any departure from the normal structure of the chemicals, perhaps involving movement of the bonded nuclei closer together or further apart (i.e. 'stretching' or 'compressing' their bonds), is linked to a rise in energy. So it takes energy to disturb the electrons and nuclei of nitrogen and hydrogen from their normal balanced and stable arrangements. The energy needed to cause such disturbance can come from collisions between molecules, collisions in which the kinetic energy bringing the molecules together can serve to raise the chemicals concerned some way up the energy 'slopes' around the energy 'well' of the diagram.

Relatively gentle collisions, which disturb the chemicals' electron arrangements only a little, correspond to moving just a little way up from the bottom of the energy well. The second law of thermodynamics ensures that the extra energy is soon dispersed into the surroundings as the chemicals fall back down into the stable states corresponding to the bottom of the well. Stable states are stable simply *because* they are at the bottom of energy wells, meaning that they correspond to electronic structures that chemicals tend to adopt as they lose energy into their surroundings.

There are two energy wells in the diagram, however, representing two stable states which two nitrogen atoms and six hydrogen atoms can adopt. The bottom of the other energy well corresponds to the totally rearranged structure in which the atoms adopt the form of two ammonia molecules rather than one nitrogen and three hydrogen molecules. The nitrogen and hydrogen molecules can be induced to undergo this rearrangement if they collide with sufficient energy to 'push them' all the way up to the peak of the curve in the diagram. Reaching this peak requires considerable change of chemical structure, of electron arrangement in other words, and that requires a considerable input of energy. When the chemicals reach the top of the energy hill, they are in a very unstable state, since the slightest change in structure will lead them down one or other side of the energy hill. Either route can be taken. In other words, the chemicals may slide back into the energy well they came from, to adopt once more the form of nitrogen and hydrogen, or they may fall down into the new stable structure of ammonia molecules. If we begin with a mixture of pure nitrogen and hydrogen, and raise the temperature enough to ensure that some collisions will be violent enough to push these chemicals into the state represented by the top of the energy hill, then inevitably some ammonia is going to be formed. We will see a chemical reaction proceed, in which nitrogen and hydrogen will react to create ammonia.

All chemical reactions can be represented by the movement of chemicals between the energy wells that correspond to relatively stable structures that are likely to survive long enough for us to detect and examine them. The structures at the top of the energy hills between these stable states are unstable 'intermediate' structures, which can be so short-lived that they are very difficult to study, and in many cases very little is known about them. The energy needed to raise the energy of chemicals up to the highest energy intermediate state of any reaction is called the 'activation energy' of the reaction, since it is the energy needed to activate the otherwise stable chemicals into reaction.

One other energy change is very important, namely the overall change in the energy of the chemicals during the course of the reaction. This is the difference between the bottom of the starting materials energy well, and the bottom of the products energy well. In the example of figure 12.1a the structure of the products (ammonia molecules) corresponds to an inherently lower energy structure than the structures of the starting materials, so energy is going to be given out to the surroundings, overall, during the course of this reaction. Initially the excess energy will probably be stored within the ammonia molecules, but it will soon be jostled away into the surroundings by the effect of collisions between these newly formed molecules and the other particles around them.

It is vital to realize that the overall release of energy during a chemical reaction, although very common, is not a general rule of chemistry. Many reactions take place in which the products correspond to higher energy structures than the starting materials. We must examine such situations now, to see how they can fit with the requirements of the second law of thermodynamics. We can do so using the same reaction because, and this is another vital point, *all chemical reactions are, in principle, reversible.*

Just as nitrogen and hydrogen can undergo a reaction to form ammonia, so ammonia molecules can act as the starting materials of the reverse reaction, in which nitrogen and hydrogen are generated. All that is required is for them to be supplied with sufficient energy to move up their side of the energy hill of figure 12.1a, to attain the unstable transition state which can either give rise to ammonia again, or nitrogen and hydrogen molecules. In this case, the activation energy of the reverse reaction is considerably larger than that of the forward reaction, but ammonia molecules can and do react to generate nitrogen and hydrogen.

So if all reactions are reversible, what determines the direction of a chemical reaction? The answer is the tendency of energy to disperse towards an even distribution; but that needs some further explanation. Suppose we begin with a mixture of nitrogen and hydrogen, choosing conditions of temperature and pressure under which the forward reaction can proceed. At first, there is no ammonia present, so the reverse reaction is impossible. The formation of ammonia will proceed for a while, with the energy released during the process being dispersed into the mixture of nitrogen, hydrogen and ammonia gases. We will assume the mixture is in a thoroughly insulated vessel, so that no heat loss is possible. As soon as some ammonia has formed, the reverse reaction becomes a possibility if sufficient energy disperses *into* the ammonia molecules due to their very violent collision with other molecules. At first, the reverse reaction may only proceed to a negligible extent, because there are so few ammonia molecules and the molecules of the mixture may not be colliding with sufficient kinetic energy; but all the time more ammonia is being formed, and the energy released by that process is raising the temperature of the mixture. Both these factors, increased numbers of ammonia molecules and increased temperature, increase the likelihood of the violent collisions in which enough energy disperses back into ammonia molecules to make them react to form nitrogen and hydrogen. At the same time, the nitrogen and hydrogen is being used up by the forward reaction, and the likelihood of the forward reaction suffers as a result. The rate of the reverse reaction will steadily increase as the rate of the forward reaction falls, until finally both rates will be equal. In this eventual 'equilibrium' state, both reactions continue, but at the same rate. A chemical deadlock has been reached because the energy of the system has become as evenly dispersed as is possible. It is just as likely that energy will disperse into ammonia to generate nitrogen and hydrogen, as it is that it will disperse out of nitrogen and hydrogen during the generation of ammonia.

All reactions are reversible, and all will settle down into the deadlock of equilibrium if given enough time, but there are two important things to bear in mind when interpreting that statement. First, a reaction may take such a long time to settle down into the equilibrium position, that for a long time it will appear to be proceeding in one direction only; and second, the quantities of the chemicals on each side of the reaction equation may be very unbalanced at the equilibrium position. For example, equilibrium may only be reached when there is a ten thousand to one imbalance of 'products' over starting 'materials', so if one had begun with pure starting materials, then for practical purposes one would observe a one-way and virtually complete conversion of these starting materials into the products. Nonetheless, the important point that all reactions are reversible, even if the reverse reactions are very unlikely, is a vital one to comprehend. In some cases, the reversibility is very obvious because equilibrium is reached with significant amounts of 'starting materials' and 'products present'. In other cases the reversibility of a reaction may be very hard to detect – but it is always there.

Notice that I have begun to put 'starting materials' and 'products' in inverted commas. This is because the starting materials of the reaction moving in one direction are clearly the products of the reaction moving in the other direction, and vice versa. The equation

$$N_2 + 3H_2 \rightarrow 2NH_3$$

could quite legitimately be written

$$2NH_3 \rightarrow N_2 + 3H_2$$

and is actually best written as

$$N_2 + 3H_2 \rightleftharpoons 2NH_3$$

or

$$2NH_3 \rightleftharpoons N_2 + 3H_2$$

with the double arrows indicating that reaction in either direction is possible. Which direction dominates depends on the precise conditions, such as temperature and pressure, under which the reaction occurs, and these conditions can be adjusted to make either reaction the dominant one, meaning that one can arrange for the equilibrium state to contain an excess of either nitrogen and hydrogen, or of ammonia, depending on the conditions chosen.

So there are two further vital points to add to our developing overview of chemistry: reactions which take in energy, to generate products of higher energy than the starting materials, can occur whenever the tendency of energy to disperse takes that energy into the reacting chemicals rather than out of them; and all reactions are reversible, although there can be great differences in the likelihood, and therefore the rate, of the forward and reverse reactions.

So we can now bring all of the foundations of chemistry together into one brief summarizing list:

Chemical reactions occur when moving atoms and/or molecules and/or ions collide with one another to cause a rearrangement of the electrons in these particles.

The electron rearrangement can involve the breaking of some existing chemical bonds, and the making of new chemical bonds.

Energy is required to initiate the electron rearrangement, but energy is later given out as the chemicals settle down into their new arrangements; and *overall*, energy can either be given out from the reacting chemicals or taken in by them during the course of a reaction, depending on the chemicals involved.

All reactions are reversible, although in many cases reaction in one direction is much more likely than in the other direction;

and as reactions proceed they automatically favour the direction which leads to an increased dispersal of the energy of the universe towards a more even distribution.

Chemical reactions are what happens to chemicals as they are forced, by the automatic dispersal of energy towards a more even distribution, to adjust their energy levels to levels that are compatible with the energy of their surroundings.

That could be described as the pure essence of chemistry, but of course in distilling out the essence we are forced to discard much complexity and subtlety. Let me make amends for some of the distillation losses, before we move on to the examine the chemical processes of life in chapter 13.

An energy profile diagram such as figure 12.1a gives a very oversimplified view of the course of a chemical reaction. It tends to make us think that the reaction which forms ammonia is initiated by the simultaneous collision of one nitrogen molecule and three hydrogen molecules, to generate a single high energy intermediate, containing two nitrogen atoms and six hydrogen atoms, which then breaks up into two ammonia molecules. This is certainly not the case. In the first place, the simultaneous collision of four molecules is far too improbable an event to be the initiator of a chemical reaction. The crucial initiating step of the reaction is probably the collision between a single nitrogen and a single hydrogen molecule. This would generate an initial intermediate which would then react further, via a large number of different steps. Chemical reactions which can be summarized *overall* by nice neat equations usually proceed in a complicated stepwise manner involving many high energy and unstable intermediates. This can be indicated in an approximate way by a diagram such as figure 12.1b, which indicates several shallow energy wells on the way up and down the main energy hill, each corresponding to a short-lived intermediate state.

Figure 12.1a may also suggest to you that there are only two ways in which the structure of any chemical can change, corresponding to movement to the left or to the right along the horizontal axis. A three-dimensional 'reaction landscape' with both horizontal axes representing changes in chemical structure would be much more accurate. The chemicals that we see and use in the everyday world occupy the bottoms of the wells in such a landscape; chemical reactions involve chemicals being jostled between wells by the energy of their collisions (or some other input of energy, such as a burst of electromagnetic radiation), and the slopes and peaks in the landscape correspond to the high energy intermediates that have only a fleeting existence during the course of chemical reactions. In such a three-dimensional landscape there are clearly many different ways in which the structure of a chemical can be altered (corresponding to movement up different parts of the walls of the energy wells), and each chemical or mixture of chemicals can clearly participate in several different reactions (each one represented by movement into a different well). Even such a landscape, of course, is only an analogy or 'model' of the real situation, but it can give us a nice impression of the energy changes involved in chemical reactions, and of the various possibilities for chemical change and restrictions on that change.

The final complexity we shall consider involves the well-known phenomenon of the 'catalysis' of chemical reactions. Many reactions, including the ammonia-forming reaction chosen as our example above, proceed rather slowly when the reactants are simply mixed and left to their own devices. Almost all reactions can be made to proceed more quickly by the addition of some other chemical which acts as a 'catalyst' of the reaction. A catalyst is a substance which speeds up a reaction while itself remaining unchanged overall. Catalysts achieve their effects by opening up new routes, or 'mechanisms', for reactions to follow, routes which involve a lower activation energy than the routes otherwise available. Since a catalyst lowers the activation energy of a reaction, it means that a larger proportion of the reactants will have sufficient kinetic energy to react when they collide, and hence the reaction will proceed more quickly than it would in the absence of the catalyst.

Catalysts are essential to make most of the reactions exploited by the chemical industry work in an efficient and economic manner. A catalyst of finely divided iron, combined with small quantities of various other chemicals, allows the manufacture of ammonia to proceed fast enough for it to serve as a basic feed reaction of the fertilizer industry. Without the help of the catalyst, nitrogen-containing fertilizers could not be made in anything like their current quantities, and they would be much more expensive. Catalysts of rhodium and platinum metal are used in the 'catalytic converters' fitted to some cars to clean up their exhaust emissions. These catalysts speed up a range of reactions which convert noxious mixtures of unburnt fuel, carbon monoxide and nitrogen oxides into the less harmful chemicals carbon dioxide, water and nitrogen. Natural catalysts called 'enzymes' catalyse all of the chemical reactions within our bodies that keep us alive – but that is a subject for the next chapter rather than this one.

The world of chemistry is full of many more details and complexities that occupy many large volumes on library shelves; yet the essence of all that complexity is very simple, as summarized on page 118. Remember that all of the pushing and pulling and rearranging of electrons and nuclei that takes place as chemistry proceeds is the result of the electromagnetic force that strains to force particles with the same sign of charge apart, and particles with opposite charges together; and remember also that chemical changes are given direction, overall, by the tendency of the energy of chemicals to disperse towards a more even distribution.

So, chemistry is a frantic dance of particles in which some participants are drawn towards one another while others are forcefully repelled, with the whirling energy of the dance defying these ordering forces as it spreads across the dance-floor!

13 Life

Life is the phenomenon of Nature whose nature we most dearly wish to understand; yet nobody understands life fully, for the most significant aspect of life is the conscious mind which exists within each human skull; and nobody knows how that mind is created and sustained, or even what it is. A great deal is known, however, about the inner mechanisms of living things, mechanisms which maintain the cells that form such organs as your heart, lungs and the brain which somehow creates, or at least sustains, your conscious thoughts. The basic nature of life's inner mechanisms is chemical. Living things appear to be marvellously intricate chemical machines. I should be careful here – there may be more to us than 'mere chemistry', especially since the origin of our consciousness and our thoughts remains a mystery, but all that has been discovered within us so far is chemical machinery. In this chapter we shall take a look at the main components of that machinery to discover how it allows us, and all other living things, to live.

As you look into a complex living thing such as a human or other animal, or a common plant, you soon discover that it is composed of many smaller living units called 'cells'. The living cell is the fundamental unit of life. The simplest living things are single cells, while the most complex are assemblies of enormous numbers of cells. So the differences between different living things boil down to differences in the types and numbers of cells they contain. An amoeba is a well-known type of 'free-living' single cell which does little else but move around, take in food and use it to grow and then multiply by dividing in two. A human is a conglomeration of around ten trillion cells, of which there are many different types each specialized to do different things; and the interaction of these cells allows a human to think and talk and be aware of its own existence.

Although cells can differ enormously in what they do and what they look like, they all share a common core of essential features which let them work. Figure 13.1 outlines these features, using a cell from a 'higher organism' such as ourselves as an a example. The simplest cells of all are the cells of so-called 'lower organisms' such as bacteria, but although they have a slightly different structure (lacking a separate 'nucleus', for example), the basic chemistry that makes them work is very similar. It is important to remember that all of the things shown in figure 13.1 and described in the following

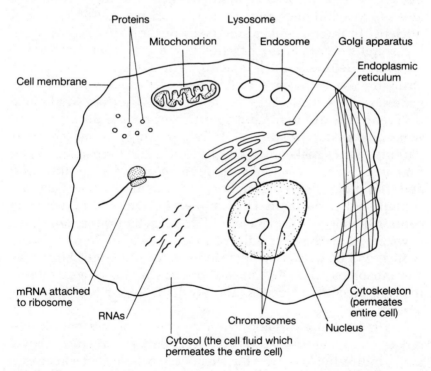

Figure 13.1 A highly schematic view of the most essential features of an animal cell.

text are chemicals (or conglomerates of different chemicals) composed of atoms and/or molecules and/or ions. So all of the changes and interactions I will describe occur because they are essentially chemical reactions driven by the tendency of energy to disperse throughout the universe.

All cells are surrounded by a thin 'cell membrane', composed of chemicals which isolate the contents of the cell from the outside world, although they do allow the selective passage of some chemicals into and out of the cell. The interior of the cell itself is a watery 'ocean' known as the cell cytosol. The chemistry of life occurs within a watery solution, probably because life first arose and then evolved within the waters on the surface of the earth.

The cells of higher organisms have other membranes within them, which separate some regions of the cell into 'cells within the cell' which are known as organelles. The most important and universal of such membrane-bound organelles is the cell nucleus. In the nucleus, at the heart of the living cell, we find the secret treasure at the heart of all life – the chemical known as DNA (deoxyribonucleic acid), which contains within its structure the things we call 'genes'. As most people know, genes are the chemical agents of heredity. They are what make different cells different, and so different people different, and what make the offspring of living things resemble their parents. Genes make mice look like mice and humans look like humans. Genes are actually distinct regions of incredibly long and thin molecules of DNA. Some organisms, such as bacteria, contain only one main DNA molecule, while our own cells contain 46 massive molecules of DNA. Each of these molecules is wrapped up together with various types of protein molecule (which will be discussed later) to form the structures known as chromosomes. The DNA of each of our chromosomes contains many thousands of genes, and we have about 100,000 genes overall.

The importance of genes, in a very general and descriptive sense, is as follows: their precise chemical structure allows them, indirectly, to control the chemical reactions that construct a living organism from non-living chemical raw materials; and their structure also allows them to become copied to generate the new copies needed to give rise to new generations of life. This is sometimes expressed by saying that genes carry the 'genetic information' needed to generate life. This 'information' can be thought of as the 'instructions' needed to generate specific members of another class of chemicals known as proteins, because the true importance of genes is that they allow the manufacture of specific protein molecules to occur within a cell. Such terms as genetic 'information' and 'instructions' should not be taken too literally, however; all that really happens is that various chemicals interact in specific ways which eventually give rise to the chemical phenomenon we call life.

Ignoring a few exceptions and complexities for the moment, I can say that one gene is a section of a DNA molecule that is able to generate one specific protein molecule. The full complement of genes embodied in a cell's DNA is known as the cell's genome, and each of our own 100,000 or so genes is believed to be present in virtually every cell of our bodies. The genome of a human, in other words, corresponds to the genome of one of its cells.

If the importance of genes is that they give rise to proteins, the next big question must be what do proteins do? Proteins perform a very wide range of essential tasks within living things, but there is a sweet simplicity at the heart of the seeming variety and complexity of their effects. Proteins, due to their chemical structure, have the ability to *selectively bind* to specific chemicals, and then either to perform an act of *catalysis*, which means the encouragement of some chemical reaction involving the chemicals they bind to, or themselves to undergo a specific *conformational change* which then brings about some other specific chemical effect. Selective binding, catalysis and conformational change are the three great tasks performed by proteins, and we shall need to investigate them further to illustrate why these three effects are so important.

The most vital and influential role played by the proteins is to act as the molecules that actually construct and maintain all cells. The proteins that do the job of cell construction and maintenance are known as 'enzymes', and they perform their seemingly miraculous task in a very simple way. Each enzyme is a very specific chemical catalyst (with the proper definition of a catalyst, remember, being something that *speeds up* a particular chemical reaction while itself remaining unchanged in the process). I have already said that living things are chemical machines, which implies that the overall activities of a living organism are the net result of many interacting chemical reactions. Now, countless different chemical reactions *could*, in principle, take place between the many chemicals found inside cells, given enough time and opportunity. Most of these countless possible reactions would not help create life and would in many cases destroy it. So for life to assemble out of all that varied chemical potential, something must encourage the reactions that will integrate to generate life, while preventing or at least in no way assisting those reactions that would not create life, and might even destroy it. This is the task performed by enzymes, as summarized in figure 13.2. Enzymes catalyse the chemical reactions of life, each enzyme catalysing one, or at most a few, specific reactions; and their acts of catalysis ensure that only the right reactions proceed in the right places at the right times at suitable speeds and in the correct order.

Each of the thousands of chemical reactions that combine to make an amoeba, a mouse or a human, is catalysed by a particular enzyme. Without the help of enzymes many of these reactions would never proceed to any significant extent. Enzymes make the intricately integrated chemistry of life possible. They generate order, structure and balance out of the messy chemical soup within our cells.

So by containing the information needed to make enzymes and other proteins, genes ultimately determine the structure and activities of all cells and organisms; but the genes are only important because they determine what proteins a living thing contains.

The overall message of this first section of the chapter is that life is based on cells containing genes that direct the manufacture of proteins, which act together to construct the chemistry of life from available raw materials. Before delving more deeply into the activities of the crucial genes and proteins, we must briefly consider one other class of chemical – RNA. RNA

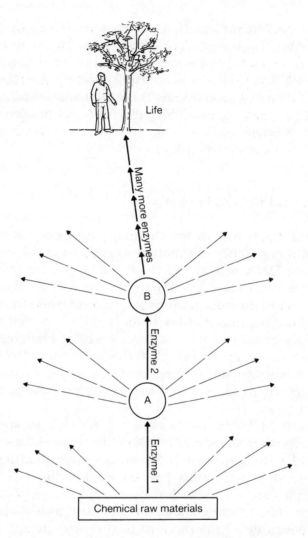

Figure 13.2 By selectively catalysing some chemical reactions (bold arrows), while giving no help at all to many other possible reactions (dashed arrows), enzymes channel the chemical potential of the environment along the narrow chemical paths that lead to life.

(ribonucleic acid) has a very similar structure to DNA, and it acts as a 'working copy' of the DNA of a gene, a copy which travels out from the cell nucleus and into the cytosol where protein assembly actually proceeds. DNA is the master copy of a cell's genetic information, which stays secure in the nucleus. RNA copies of the DNA of each gene are made in the nucleus, to be transported out into the cytosol when required; and it is these RNA copies of a gene that actually physically direct the manufacture of proteins. As their full names imply, both RNA and DNA belong to a class of chemicals known as 'nucleic acids'. Nucleic acids are the chemicals whose structure determines the chemistry of life.

Genes and the double-helix

Right at the centre of the chemistry of life is the DNA which stores the genetic information needed to make and control a cell. For DNA to serve as a carrier of genetic information it must be able to do two main things. First, it obviously must be able to contain information; and second, there must be some way for this information to be copied, so that when cells multiply by dividing in two a copy will be available for each of the two new cells. If we look at the structure of DNA, and then look at ways to simplify and generalize the features of a very complex chemical, we will soon discover how it meets these two criteria.

Figure 13.3A is as close as we can get to showing in a diagram what DNA really 'looks' like. It shows a short section of DNA with spheres of different sizes and shading representing the different atoms present in the chemical. Real DNA molecules are many thousands of times longer than this short section, but to understand the chemical as a whole we need only consider a little piece of it. A single gene drawn on the same scale as figure 13.3A, would be at least six metres long (for many genes, much longer). DNA is made out of only five different types of atom: hydrogen, carbon, nitrogen, oxygen and phosphorus atoms. Although that is quite a small number of different types of atoms, the structure of DNA still looks very complex when all of its atoms are shown. Fortunately, it can readily be simplified, and one of the simplifying features is visible, though not obvious, in figure 13.3A. Two helical ribbons of atoms can be seen spiralling around a central inner

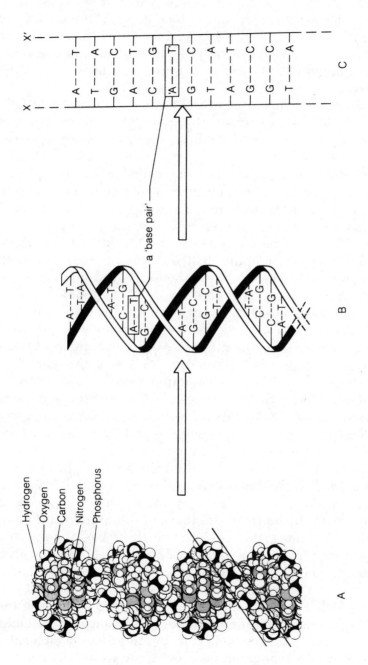

Figure 13.3 The structure of the DNA double-helix.

core (part of one of them is highlighted by the two straight lines drawn on either side of it in the figure). These are known as the helical 'backbones' of DNA, since the only real purpose they serve is as a framework holding the atoms of the inner core, and together they are the origin of the famous 'double-helix' structure of DNA.

The double-helical nature of DNA is seen much more clearly in figure 13.3B. This considerably simplifies the structure of DNA by distinguishing clearly between its two main regions – helical backbones and central core – and representing them schematically rather than showing every atom. The helical backbones have a constant repeating structure that is identical from one piece of DNA to another, from one gene to another, so the helical backbones cannot be where the genetic information lies. The information must lie in the central core, which has been simplified in figure 13.3B by replacing the atoms with the first initial of the different chemical groupings that are present in the core. The core of a DNA double-helix is composed of only four different chemical groups known as 'bases'. These bases are 'adenine' (A), 'thymine' (T), 'guanine' (G) and 'cytosine' (C). The differences between different DNA molecules, and so the differences between the genes of amoebae, mice and humans, simply involve the different sequences in which the four bases of DNA are arranged. So to understand how DNA works, we now only have to worry about the four bases – A, T, G and C – and the order in which they occur within the core of a double-helix.

In figure 13.3C the simplification process has been taken one final step. The helical backbones have been untwisted and are now represented by straight lines. This allows us to concentrate on the central bases that carry the genetic information. This diagram makes it clear that these bases are strung out in an ordered array on the helical backbones, and that each base on one helix is opposite another base on the other helix; but notice that there are dotted lines between the bases of opposing helices, rather than solid lines. This is because the DNA double-helix, although commonly referred to as the DNA molecule, is not really one molecule, but two distinct molecules wound around one another. Each helix and its attached bases, each 'strand' of the double-helix in other words, is a single discrete molecule. The two helices are wound around one another, and held together by weak intermolecular attractions, of the type discussed on page 105, rather than by full chemical bonds. So the double helix is in fact a double molecule, with each individual molecule held to the other by an array of weak electromagnetic attractions between pairs of opposing bases, known as 'base-pairs'. Strictly speaking, the individual helices are not even true molecules, but are molecular ions, since negatively electrically charged ionic groups are studded along the outside of each helical backbone.

In only two steps we have reduced the structure of double-helical DNA from the real-life assembly of five types of atom to a simple array of letters (representing the four chemical groups we call bases), lines (representing the rest of the DNA) and dashed lines (representing the weak bonds between opposing bases). The structure of this simple array contains the secret of how DNA can serve as the genetic material of life.

The first step towards uncovering the secret is to search for the hidden order present in the structure of DNA. It is not very well hidden, but it might escape a first glance. Take a look at the specific bases that make up individual base-pairs. Wherever an A appears on one strand it is paired with a T on the other strand, and wherever there is a T its partner is an A. The same applies to all the Gs and Cs: each G is paired up with a C of the other strand, and each C is paired with a G. These are known as the rules of base-pairing, and they result from the three-dimensional chemical structures of the bases. Throughout all of the DNA of any cell there are only two types of base-pair – As and Ts paired together, and Gs and Cs paired together – although the two types of base-pair can appear either way round. These are the only base-pairs that can fit together within the double-helical structure, and they are described as pairs between 'complementary' bases, A and T being complementary, as are G and C. Any two DNA strands whose base sequences match according to the rules of base-pairing are complementary strands, and only such complementary DNA strands can bind together to form a DNA double-helix. The phenomenon of base-pairing between specific complementary bases is the key to all of DNA's activities; and remember, the phenomenon of specific base-pairing is simply an automatic chemical consequence of the structure of the bases involved.

Let us now return to the two things that DNA must do, to see how the phenomenon of specific base-pairing allows it to do them. DNA must somehow be *copied*, to provide copies for future generations, which boils down to the need to provide a copy for each of the two cells formed when a cell multiplies by splitting in two; and DNA must somehow be able to *contain information* – the information needed to direct the manufacture of specific protein molecules.

The answer to the copying problem stares you in the face as you examine figure 13.3C. The structure of DNA makes it very easy to produce faithful copies of any particular double-helix, because *all the information needed to make an entire double-helix is contained within either of its two strands*. To appreciate this, imagine the two strands of a model of the double-helix were pulled apart and you were supplied with only one of them. Provided you were also given a supply of the four bases linked to the atoms that form the helical backbone, you could readily reconstruct the original double-helix. You would simply need to link together a new strand with the bases paired up according to the rules of base-pairing (see figure 13.4). This is very close to what happens in living cells when their DNA is 'replicated' (to use the accepted term for the copying process). The DNA becomes unwound by the activity of various proteins, able to bind to DNA and catalyse the unwinding; and then other proteins act as the enzymes that catalyse the reactions which link the required new bases and backbone atoms into two new helices, one complementary to each of the original separated strands (see figure 13.5).

Although enzymes catalyse all of the chemical reactions involved in DNA replication, the specificity of the process is due to the structure of the bases of DNA. The correct base-pairs are formed simply because these are the only ones that can form in a way that allows the available enzymes to link the new bases into a growing DNA chain. If the wrong bases should pair up, something which can happen, they will be in

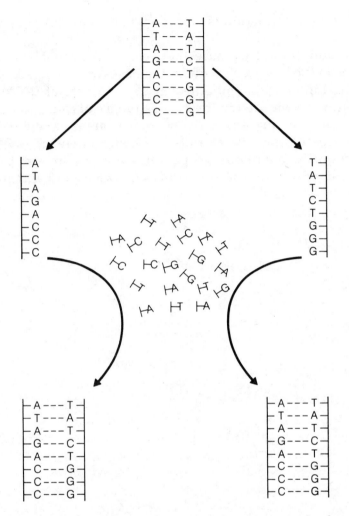

Figure 13.4 Anyone provided with only one strand of a DNA double-helix and a supply of nucleotides (bases linked to atoms that form the 'backbone' of the DNA) could easily re-create the original double-helix by following the rules of base-pairing.

the wrong position for the linkage reaction to occur – that is why they are 'wrong'.

So we have seen the answer to the copying problem and it is wonderfully simple. The answer to the information problem is also simple, in essence, but rather more complex in the details of how the information is 'decoded' to create working protein molecules.

The only thing that varies between different DNA double-helices is the *sequence* in which the bases are arranged. So the genetic information embodied in the structure of DNA must somehow be encoded in the base sequence of DNA. A double-helix can contain any base sequence at all, provided the sequences of the two strands are complementary, so there is obviously enormous scope for variation in the precise structure of different sections of DNA. The way in which such

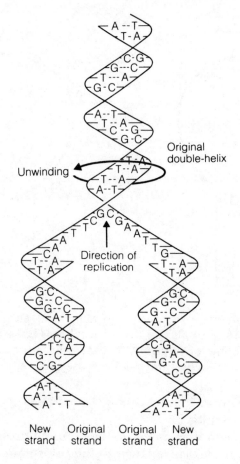

Figure 13.5 The replication of double-helical DNA.

variations in base sequence can encode the information needed to generate specific proteins becomes more obvious when we examine the chemical structure of proteins.

Figure 13.6 gives us a good impression of what a protein molecule actually 'looks like', illustrating a protein in which all the individual atoms are represented by spheres. It reveals nothing, however, of the simplicity that lies hidden within such apparent structural complexity. We can soon reveal that simplicity, just as we did for DNA, by replacing the individual atoms by diagrammatic representations of the various chemical groups that combine to make a protein. All proteins are long chain-like molecules, as shown in figure 13.7C, made by the linking together of many smaller molecules called 'amino acids' which are represented by rectangles in the figure. Each amino acid is composed of between 10 and 27 atoms, and 20 different amino acids are found in proteins, although most proteins contain several hundred amino acids altogether.

Once a protein has been made by the linkage of the correct amino acids in the correct sequence (a process catalysed by enzymes, of course), then the long protein chain usually folds up into a highly specific shape, represented schematically by figure 13.7C and more realistically by figure 13.6. Only once a protein has adopted its final folded form can it actually perform its chemical role, such as acting as an enzyme able to speed up some specific chemical reaction. It is crucial to realize, however, that the nature of this folding process is determined entirely by the amino acids in the protein chain and the sequence in which they are arranged. The protein is automatically pushed and pulled into its final folded structure by electromagnetic forces of attraction and repulsion between the amino acids of the protein and the watery environment within the cell. So once the correct amino acids have been linked together in the correct sequence, the job of making a protein is essentially complete. The protein chain will then fold up into the precise three-dimensional structure that the electromagnetic force pulls it into; and this will be the structure that allows it to perform its highly specific biological task.

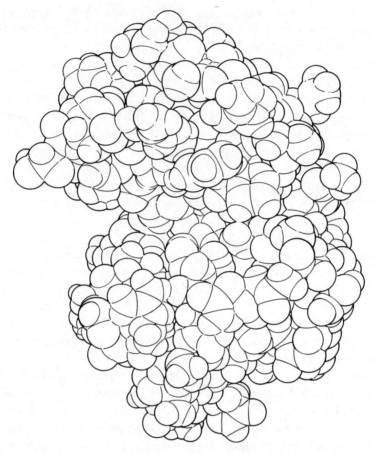

Figure 13.6 A protein molecule. (Based on a photograph by R. J. Feldmann, Division of Computer Research and Technology, US National Institutes of Health.)

So the role performed by genetic information begins to look simpler and clearer: the genetic information that directs the manufacture of a protein takes the form of a linear sequence of bases in DNA, and what that information must do is determine the linear sequence in which a series of amino acids becomes linked together. A linear sequence of bases on DNA somehow determines the linear sequence of amino acids in a protein. So to know the essence of the way in which DNA controls protein manufacture we merely need to know the relationship between the base sequence of the gene that 'codes for' a protein and the amino acid sequence of the protein it encodes. The answer can be stated very simply: each sequence of three bases in DNA can direct one particular amino acid to become linked up into a growing protein chain.

That single sentence summarizes a wondrous and complex process whose full details are not yet known, but the next few pages will examine, in briefest outline, what is known about this central mechanism of life. A diagrammatic summary can be found in figure 13.7A–B.

It begins with DNA – the master copy of a cell's genetic information. Remember that a section of DNA encoding one particular protein is called a gene, and the first thing that happens when a gene gives rise to a protein is that a copy of the gene is made in the form of RNA. There are two obvious differences between the DNA of a gene and its RNA working copy. First, the RNA is single-stranded. It is a replica of just one strand of the double-stranded DNA (the RNA in the figure is a replica of the left-hand strand of the unwound double-helix). Also, wherever the base T appears in DNA, a different base, known as 'U' (for uracil), appears in its RNA copy. Uracil is very similar in structure to thymine, i.e. T, and it forms a base pair with adenine (A) just as thymine does. So for our purposes the bases U in RNA and T in DNA can be regarded as behaving identically.

The RNA replica of one strand of the double-helix is made in much the same way as new copies of DNA itself. The two strands of a portion of the double-helix become temporarily unwound, allowing enzymes to use one strand (the right-hand one in figure 13.7A) as a template on which a new complementary strand of RNA can be constructed. The production of this RNA copy is known as 'transcription', since the genetic information is being transcribed from a DNA version into an RNA version, and, just like DNA replication, transcription depends on the rules of base-pairing to make it work. As transcription proceeds, the portion of double-helix that has just been transcribed becomes rewound while the next portion to be transcribed unwinds. When the RNA copy of the gene is complete it is released to do its job and the double-helix returns to its normal state.

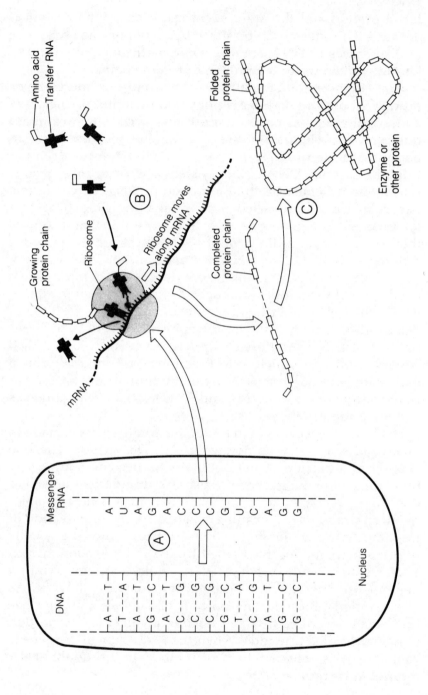

Amino acid

Transfer RNA

Growing
protein chain

Ribosome

Ribosome moves
along mRNA

mRNA

B

Messenger
RNA

A
— A
— U
— A
— G
— A
— C
— C
— C
— G
— U
— C
— A
— G
— G

DNA
A --- T
T --- A
A --- T
G --- C
A --- T
C --- G
C --- G
C --- G
G --- C
T --- A
C --- G
A --- T
G --- C
G --- C

Nucleus

Completed
protein chain

Folded
protein chain

C

Enzyme or
other protein

The RNA copy of a gene is known as 'messenger RNA', or just mRNA, since it moves from the nucleus out into the cytosol carrying its genetic message in the sequence of bases strung out along its length. The content of the message, of course, specifies the manufacture of a protein. Proteins are actually assembled on large conglomerates of protein and RNA known as 'ribosomes' which are found at various sites in the cell cytosol (see figure 13.7B). A ribosome and mRNA molecule become attached to one another through a specific chemical interaction. The ribosome then moves along the mRNA from start to finish. As it does so the protein encoded by the mRNA is assembled, because each time the ribosome encounters a sequence of three bases on the mRNA the appropriate amino acid (the one 'encoded' by the three bases) can be linked up by enzymes into the growing protein chain. That sounds a mysterious and almost magical process, but it occurs through a series of simple chemical interactions as follows.

The cytosol contains supplies of another class of RNA molecules known as 'transfer RNAs', or just tRNAs, and each tRNA molecule contains two vital parts. It contains a site at which a particular amino acid, one of the 20 found in proteins, can be attached by enzymes; and it also contains three exposed bases which can form base-pairs with three complementary bases on an mRNA molecule attached to the ribosome. So, mRNA molecules carry sets of three bases which code for the incorporation of a particular amino acid into a growing protein; and each tRNA molecule carries three bases which can bind to the complementary set of three on mRNA; and the tRNA also carries the appropriate amino acid. The sets of three

Figure 13.7 A summary of gene expression. The DNA of a gene is copied into single-stranded RNA. This messenger RNA (mRNA) moves out to the cytosol and binds to a ribosome. The ribosome moves along the mRNA, allowing appropriate transfer RNAs (tRNAs) to bind to the exposed mRNA codons by forming base-pairs between the codons and complementary anticodons on the tRNAs. Each tRNA brings with it the amino acid encoded by whichever codon the tRNA can bind to. The amino acids are linked up to form the protein encoded by the gene.

bases on mRNA, each one coding for a particular amino acid, are called 'codons', while the sets of complementary bases on tRNAs are called 'anticodons'.

So, as ribosomes travel the length of an mRNA molecule, tRNA molecules bind to the codons as they become exposed at a special site on the ribosome. Each tRNA brings with it the amino acid encoded by the exposed codon, and as these amino acids arrive they become linked together into a new protein molecule by the action of enzymes. Each tRNA is released from the ribosome once its amino acid has become incorporated into the protein chain, allowing the tRNA to be combined with another molecule of the amino acid available in the cytosol; and the ribosome moves on to expose a new codon to which a new tRNA carrying the next amino acid can bind. The details of which codons encode which amino acids are displayed in the celebrated 'genetic code' table, shown in figure 13.8.

Second base/nucleotide

		U	C	A	G	
First base/nucleotide	U	UUU UUC } Phe UUA UUG } Leu	UCU UCC UCA UCG Ser	UAU UAC } Tyr UAA STOP UAG STOP	UGU UGC } Cys UGA STOP UGG Tryp	U C A G
	C	CUU CUC CUA CUG Leu	CCU CCC CCA CCG Pro	CAU CAC } His CAA CAG } GluN	CGU CGC CGA CGG Arg	U C A G
	A	AUU AUC AUA } Ileu AUG Met	ACU ACC ACA ACG Thr	AAU AAC } AspN AAA AAG } Lys	AGU AGC } Ser AGA AGG } Arg	U C A G
	G	GUU GUC GUA GUG Val	GCU GCC GCA GCG Ala	GAU GAC } Asp GAA GAG } Glu	GGU GGC GGA GGG Gly	U C A G

(Third base/nucleotide)

Figure 13.8 The genetic code table. The amino acids specified by each codon are represented by their common abbreviations.

Eventually, the ribosome moving along the mRNA reaches a codon for which no corresponding tRNA exists. This is known as a 'stop' codon, because it signals the point at which protein manufacture is complete and so stops. The mRNA, the ribosome and the newly formed protein all dissociate from one another, leaving the protein ready to complete its folding process (the folding begins to occur as the first part of the protein is made) and begin to perform its chemical task within the cell; and leaving the ribosome and mRNA ready to enter further cycles of protein manufacture.

There you have, in briefest outline, the central chemical mechanism of life. The chemical structure of DNA determines the chemical structure of RNA, which then determines the chemical structure of a new protein molecule; and it all proceeds automatically due to a series of integrated chemical interactions and reactions catalysed by the existing enzymes of the cell.

The process of protein synthesis on the ribosome is known as 'translation' since the genetic message held in mRNA is being translated from the 'language' of DNA and RNA (i.e. from the language of nucleic acids) into the 'language' of proteins. The entire process of decoding a gene into a protein, involving both transcription and translation, is known as gene 'expression'; and it is important to remember that all of the enzymes needed to catalyse the chemistry of gene expression, and all of the other proteins involved, will have themselves been produced by the earlier expression of the genes that code for them. The chemistry of life is founded upon a mutually dependent interaction between genes and proteins: genes direct the process of protein manufacture, to generate the proteins needed to maintain and copy genes and also needed to allow the genetic information stored within the genes to be expressed. In everyday biology we are all familiar with the mutual dependency of the chicken and the egg. In molecular biology their mutual dependency is mirrored by that of the gene and the protein.

So the central mechanism of life on earth can be summarized as follows (and see also figure 14.1). Genes are long sections of DNA in which the four different bases are arranged in differing sequences. The chemical complementarity between matching base-pairs allows one DNA double-helix to be readily copied into two double-helices, which is the chemical replication process that underlies all forms of reproduction of living things. The rules of base-pairing also allow each gene to specify the manufacture of a messenger RNA molecule, which in turn specifies the manufacture of a protein. During this process the sequence of bases on the nucleic acids, DNA and then RNA, specifies the sequence in which amino acid molecules are linked up to form the new protein. The new protein folds automatically into the structure that allows it to perform its task, such as acting as an enzyme able to catalyse a chemical reaction vital to life. The differences between different organisms are a result of the different chemical reactions occurring within them, and which reactions occur depends on which proteins are encoded within the DNA of each organism's genes.

Powerful proteins

From all that has been said so far it is clear that the proteins are the vital molecular 'workers' which actually build cells and organisms, so we should give a little more consideration to the things they can do and the way in which they do them. I will quickly summarize the main roles played by the proteins of life.

First on the list are the enzymes, the proteins able to catalyse all of the chemical reactions of life. How do they achieve their astonishing feats, often increasing the rate of a chemical reaction many thousandfold while giving no help at all to a host of quite similar but undesirable reactions? In essence, the answer is very simple. In its final folded form an enzyme has grooves and clefts on its surface into which only the chemicals involved in the reaction it catalyses can fit. When bound to such 'binding sites' on an enzyme surface, the reacting chemicals are held in an orientation that makes the desired reaction much more likely than it would be without the enzyme's help. Chemical groups on the enzyme itself, belonging to the various amino acids, can participate in the reaction by pushing or pulling the electrons of the reacting chemicals in ways that encourage the reaction to proceed. Some enzymes are assisted in their catalytic wizardry by 'coenzymes', which are simple small molecules, or even by single ions of certain elements, that can bind to such enzymes to provide chemical assistance. The ability to grab hold of and utilize such coenzymes or ions is of course a result of the structure of the enzymes concerned. Some enzymes must be permanently modified by reactions catalysed by other enzymes before they can perform their tasks, but again the ability to participate in such modification reactions depends on the structures of the unmodified enzymes.

Enzymes are so ubiquitous, so important and so spectacularly efficient that it is easy to forget that proteins do a great deal of other things in addition to acting as enzymes. Apart from the enzymes, the next most fundamental class of proteins are probably the 'structural proteins' which, as their name suggests, form much of the physical structure holding cells and organisms together to give them shape and form. They can be thought of as a kind of 'molecular scaffolding' found within cells, around and in between cells.

Some such structural proteins have the special property of being able to slide past one another to create a dynamic scaffold able to move and grow larger and smaller as necessary. These are the 'contractile proteins' which give our muscles their ability to contract, and which also allow individual cells to contract and expand and move about.

Other proteins act as chemical transporters, able to bind to specific chemicals in one location and transport them to another location where they are released. Our blood contains a protein known as haemoglobin which grabs hold of the oxygen molecules in our lungs, transports them through the bloodstream, and then releases them to the cells that need oxygen. This haemoglobin is coloured deep red and is found within our red blood cells. It is the reason why these cells are red, and so why blood is red.

A large and diverse class of proteins act as chemical messengers. These are made and released in one location, and then travel to another location where they interact with the chemicals there to bring about some specific chemical effect. Many hormones, such as the 'growth hormone' that makes us grow, are either proteins or small 'mini-proteins' known as peptides.

Often these messenger proteins deliver their message by binding to members of another important class of proteins, the 'receptor' proteins, found embedded in the membrane surrounding cells. Such receptors respond to the arrival of a messenger protein by themselves initiating the chemical change within the cell that is the appropriate response to the message.

Other proteins found embedded in cell membranes are those which control the passage of chemicals into and out of cells by acting as chemical 'gates' and 'pumps'. The gates are simply channels that can open and close to allow or prevent the passage of specific chemicals; while the pumps can actively pump specific chemicals into or out of cells to build up high concentrations of these chemicals either inside or outside of the cells.

The role of many proteins is to act as the 'controllers' of other proteins or of the genes and RNAs that give rise to proteins. These proteins can bind to other proteins or RNAs or genes, and either 'activate' them, i.e. switch their chemical activities on, or 'inactivate' them, i.e. switch them off.

And finally, in this by no means comprehensive list, proteins can act as defensive weapons, able to bind to foreign organisms or diseased cells and then initiate a series of events leading to the neutralization or destruction of the 'target'. Antibodies are our most celebrated defensive proteins, but there are others.

That quick summary of the major powers of the proteins reveals how many powerful and varied things these molecular workers can do; and yet at the heart of all these diverse powers there lies great simplicity. They do it all because of the way in which their specific amino acids are arranged into specific sequences; and everything they do relies upon three general abilities – the ability to selectively bind to certain chemicals, and to then perform acts of chemical catalysis, and/or to undergo conformational changes (i.e. changes in their folded structure) which then initiate some further chemical response. Selective binding, catalysis and induced conformational change

144

are the three essential powers of the proteins that underpin everything they are able to do. What proteins do, in essence, is create cells and keep them alive and able to grow and reproduce. We have seen the central mechanism of cells, in which genes generate proteins and the proteins act as the catalysts which allow the genes to generate proteins and which also allow the genes to become replicated; but what else is there to cells, and to life?

In addition to its DNA, its RNA and its proteins, a cell contains two other main classes of components. First, it contains membranes, one of which surrounds the entire cell while others cordon off various parts of the cell into specialized 'organelles' such as the nucleus. Second, a cell contains a great range of chemicals involved in its construction and maintenance, which can be referred to collectively as 'metabolites', and which are either dissolved in the water of the cell cytosol or else appear as large insoluble agregates studded around the cell. *In essence*, there is not much more to a cell than its DNA, RNA, proteins, membranes and metabolites.

The essential nature of cellular life can be summarized as follows. Cells must take up raw materials from their surroundings, process them into the chemicals needed by the cells, excrete unwanted wastes, and keep the 'central mechanism' of DNA, RNA and protein manufacture and maintenance in operation. Enzymes catalyse every chemical step, while other proteins embedded in the cell membrane determine what can pass into a cell, and what passes out. Cells are tiny but wonderfully complex chemical machines 'devoted' to the maintenance and replication of their central DNA. Their activities have only one fundamental effect: survival and reproduction. Living things live for a while and then reproduce: that is the fundamental nature of life.

There is, however, one vital aspect of the chemistry of life that we have yet to consider – what keeps it going? Deep down at the most fundamental level you would probably expect the answer to be 'the dispersal of energy', and that indeed is the case. Just as each individual chemical process inevitably proceeds in the direction of energy dispersal, so the myriad integrated reactions of life also proceed in the direction of, and because of, energy dispersal. The inevitable tendency of energy to disperse powers your life as much as it powers the explosion of oxygen and hydrogen to create water.

Some of the chemical reactions in living things clearly proceed in the direction of energy dispersal, so there is no problem in understanding why they proceed. Much of life's chemistry, however, can seem *at first sight* to proceed in the opposite direction. What I mean by that is that many reactions in the cell convert low energy disorganized raw materials into higher energy and very organized products. This is despite the fact that the world around living things has a relatively low energy content compared to that of a living thing, making the natural direction of energy dispersal outwards rather than inwards. The chemistry of life does not violate physical and chemical law, however. Instead, reactions that might seem to move against the flow of energy dispersal are in fact just part of larger reactions which move in the direction of energy dispersal overall.

Consider a specific example. The manufacture of a protein from many amino acids is an energy-requiring process. The energy embodied within the structure of the protein, in other words, is greater than the total energy embodied within the individual amino acids. The actual reactions that link the amino acids together, however, are only a small part of the integrated chemical process that occurs on the ribosome. Other reactions of the process involve high energy chemicals breaking up into lower energy ones, and these reactions release more than enough energy to drive the protein-making process forward. This is a general rule of the chemistry of life: energy-requiring reactions are always 'chemically coupled' to other energy-releasing ones, meaning that both must occur together, and the energy-releasing reactions always release more energy than the energy-requiring reactions require. So that is how the chemistry of life proceeds without breaking the laws of physics and chemistry. The chemical reactions that sustain life are coupled together into the one complex chemical process, and that process proceeds in the direction of energy dispersal, just like everything else.

From what I have just said, it will be obvious that cells need

146

a supply of high energy chemicals in order to power energy-requiring reactions. This is one of the main functions of food, but the energy-containing chemicals of our food must get their energy from somewhere, and, ultimately, all of that energy, and so all of the energy that powers the chemistry of all life, comes from the sun.

The fundamental process that drives the chemistry of life takes place in plants, and is called photosynthesis. In photosynthesis, the radiant energy of sunlight is harnessed by a complex series of reactions to convert carbon dioxide and water into higher energy compounds called carbohydrates, and release oxygen gas as a by-product. These carbohydrates then provide the energy that powers everything else. In simplest outline, the energy is made available when the carbohydrates are combined with oxygen (the oxygen we breathe in, for example) to be converted back into carbon dioxide and water. So all life depends on the energy that disperses out from the sun, for that energy powers the chemistry that creates plants, which act as the energy-containing foodstuffs of animals, which can themselves serve as foodstuffs for other animals. Even the most committed carnivores are dependent on the energy of the sun, captured within plants, to power their lives, because without the sun's energy there would be no plants, and without plants there would be no animals, and without animals there would be no carnivores.

Overall then, life is a chemical process powered by the dispersal of energy from the sun. It proceeds automatically and inevitably as that energy strikes the earth and raises some of its chemicals up into the high energy chemical complexity of the living world.

14 Evolution

One thing is obvious to anyone contemplating the nature of life on earth: living things live for a while, and then die; but while they live they can generate newer, younger living things that live on after them. Mortality and procreation are the two most obvious aspects of life. It is less obvious, although well accepted, that as the waves of birth, life, procreation and death proceed, the nature of the living things of a population gradually changes. Thanks to these changes, the living things of one epoch can look and act completely differently from their relatives of earlier epochs. The changes power the process called 'evolution by natural selection', which is the only known process able to change the structure of living things.

To investigate the principles of evolution by natural selection we can talk in very general terms, and look at what must inevitably happen to certain 'things' with certain characteristics, regardless of whether or not we would recognize them as forms of life. So, imagine a population of things. It doesn't matter what sort of things they are provided they possess one essential ability – the ability to generate new things which are very similar to themselves but usually slightly different. Suppose that these things are surrounded by an environment containing all the raw materials needed to allow them to generate new things, although the supply of these raw materials is limited and often rather scarce. Suppose also that none of the things is immortal – each individual thing will eventually 'die' as it begins to function wrongly or falls apart due to simple 'wear and tear'. What will happen to the population of things as time passes? The simple answer is that it will evolve due to natural selection. Let's now examine closely what that means.

The existing things will make more things similar to themselves, although no two things will ever be precisely identical since their process of 'reproduction' always produces similar but slightly different versions of the existing things. Each original thing will be able to give rise to a lineage of related descendants. Old things will periodically die while the new things are being created. The population will increase or decrease depending on the difference in the rate of death and rate of reproduction.

Since no two things will be identical, some will inevitably be better at surviving and reproducing than others. Some things, in other words, will be able to survive longer than others, or reproduce faster than others, or enjoy some combination of these two advantages. Since the offspring of each thing inherit most of their progenitors' characteristics, as time passes the proportion of good survivors and reproducers in the population will increase, while the proportion of poor survivors and reproducers will decrease. In other words, those things that are good at surviving and reproducing will do just that: they will survive for long periods of time and give rise to lots of other things that can survive for long periods of time and generate lots of their own offspring in turn. Those things that are poor at surviving and reproducing will survive for only short periods of time and generate few new things, which will themselves have the same weaknesses.

So a population of reproducing and slightly varying things will gradually but inevitably become enriched in things which can survive longer and reproduce more quickly than their predecessors, and depleted of those things which can survive for only a short time and reproduce only slowly. Short-term survivors that can reproduce very quickly, or slow reproducers that survive for a very long time, might do quite well, in addition to those things that can survive for a long time and reproduce fast. The two factors of survival, time and speed of reproduction, will operate together in a perhaps complex interaction to determine how dominant any particular lineage

149

of things will become; but one thing is always certain: poor survivors and poor reproducers are doomed to suffer eventual extinction if the raw materials for reproduction are scarce.

Anyone watching and puzzling over the changes in the thing population over many generations would soon notice that the population was evolving – that is, becoming progressively enriched in more 'successful' things, where success is measured simply in terms of the ability to survive and reproduce. It would appear as if a process of selection was driving this evolution forward, with those variants that were the best survivors and reproducers being selectively preserved while the poorest survivors and reproducers were continually rejected and cast aside. But nobody is actually doing any selecting. There is no laboratory technician or God constantly reaching into the population of things to pick out and discard the poor survivors and reproducers and retain the best. There is no need for such outside intervention, because the variants that are best at surviving and reproducing will be automatically, *naturally*, selected as the dominant progenitors of future generations of things, simply because they are the things most capable of surviving and reproducing.

Natural selection is simply the preferential survival and reproduction of those things that are best at surviving and reproducing. Automatically, without any outside intervention or magic or mystery, it allows a population of things which can generate other similar but usually slightly different things to continually evolve into populations of things which are ever more efficient at surviving and reproducing.

What if the environment changes? The temperature might rise, making the things more liable to disintegrate and die; some new raw materials might suddenly become available, some which were previously in good supply might become very scarce, and so on . . . In the changed environment some of the previously very successful things might suddenly be at a great disadvantage. Some of the previously inefficient things which were coming close to extinction might suddenly find that the new environment suits them very well indeed. The requirements for success will have changed, and the population will automatically adjust in response to that change. Previously successful things which can no longer flourish will diminish in number and perhaps become extinct. Some previously rather unsuccessful things might suddenly flourish; and from the continual supply of new variant things those variants best able to survive and reproduce in the new environment will survive and reproduce and come to represent an increasing proportion of the evolving thing population.

Changes in the environment will continually affect the population of things, while the activities of the things will continually affect the environment. A dynamic inter-relationship will exist between the thing population and the environment, each one affecting the changes of the other. That is the essence of evolution by natural selection within a population of things. Now we must abandon our abstract notion of things and turn to the real things that matter to the evolution of life – the single cells and multicellular plants and animals that are the living things of the planet. The dogma of modern biology tells us that these living things have arisen from earlier generations of living things by a process of evolution driven by natural selection. We must consider a few of the details of how that evolution can happen.

Living things can certainly 'generate new things which are very similar to themselves but usually slightly different'. That is what happens every time a living thing reproduces, and it is the basic requirement for evolution by natural selection. Living things make other similar living things thanks to the ability of one DNA double-helix to undergo the process of replication that creates two new daughter double-helices. Such DNA replication allows the genome of one cell to generate the genomes needed by two cells, allowing the original cell to multiply by dividing into two. Ultimately, it allows the genome of one human, or other animal or plant, to give rise to the genomes of new generations of offspring.

So DNA replication is the central process that allows living things to make more living things, but where does the necessary variation enter the process? Somehow the genomes of living things must be able to undergo the changes which are needed to create the variety which powers evolution. Any change in genetic material, which usually means a change in the structure of DNA, can be described as a 'mutation'. There are many different ways in which mutations can be generated. Remember that an organism's genome is embodied in the sequence in which the four bases of DNA are arranged throughout an organism's DNA. Mutations involve some alteration of that base sequence.

The simplest type of mutation involves a change to a single base. This may involve one base being replaced by a different one, or one base being deleted from the base sequence of DNA, or a new base being added. Simple mutations of this type can be generated by the action of 'mutagenic' chemicals upon DNA, or by exposure to radiation, or they can be generated when random mistakes are made during the replication of DNA. The chemistry of life is not perfect – occasionally things go wrong and mistakes occur.

Many of the other changes which can be inflicted upon genetic material are catalysed by various enzymes, but most are best regarded as occasional mistakes brought about by the activity of enzymes able to cut and reseal DNA. Such events allow large sections of DNA to become duplicated, deleted, or turned around ('inverted'). Sometimes long sections of DNA can even break loose to wander freely for a while before becoming reincorporated into the main DNA at a different location. All of these processes allow genetic material to change slightly as it passes from generation to generation, causing the reproduction of living things to generate new creatures very similar to their parents, but almost always slightly different.

Further scope for variety is available in creatures such as ourselves, which reproduce through the sexual union of DNA from two individuals. When the sperm cell of a male unites with the egg cell of a female, the DNA of both individuals combines to create the genome of the fertilized egg that will grow and divide to generate their child. So the offspring of sexually reproducing organisms inherit genetic material from two parents, and this inheritance happens in such a way that the same two parents can generate an almost infinite variety of different children depending on which parts of their genetic material are passed on into the fertilized egg cell that becomes their child.

This is not the place to go into great detail (you will find more details in my own book *Vital Principles – The Molecular Mechanisms of Life*, or in any basic biology text). For the purposes of this book the essential principles are sufficient, and the essential principles behind the reproduction and evolution of life are that living things can multiply thanks to the replication of DNA, and living populations can evolve because the structure of DNA can change to give rise to new variant individuals to be put to the test of natural selection (see figure 14.1). Natural selection is believed to be the

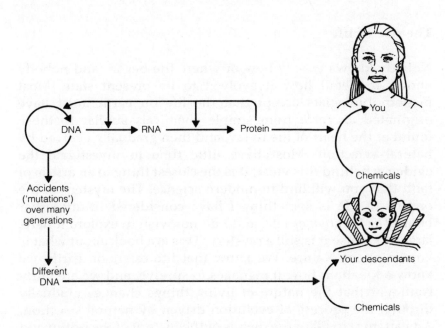

Figure 14.1 Basic life and evolution. DNA makes RNA which makes the proteins that catalyse the creation and maintenance of you, as well as catalysing the creation and maintenance of your DNA, RNA and protein. Future generations are generated by the replication of DNA, catalysed by proteins; and mutations altering the DNA provide the different DNA needed to allow different forms of life to evolve by natural selection.

mechanism which allows physics and chemistry to create the intricate complexity of life. The basic instructions for making living things are encoded in a sequence of chemical bases represented by the letters A, T, G and C. Modifications to the structure of living things correspond to changes in the base sequence of their DNA; and if these modifications create organisms that are better at surviving and reproducing than existing forms, then the new forms will flourish; while if they are poorer and weaker, they will soon die out.

These are the mechanisms of evolution. Let's now look at its main effects.

The rise of life

Nobody knows exactly how or where life began, and nobody knows in detail how it evolved to its present state. Most modern biologists accept that the life on earth must have originated *on earth* from simple chemicals similar to those found at the heart of life today, and then gradually evolved by natural selection. Most have little time to investigate the evidence behind this view; it is the closest thing to an article of faith that you will find in modern science. The mystery of the origins of life is something I have considered in an earlier book, *The Creation of Life*, and I do not wish to explore it here, largely because it is still a mystery. This is a book about what is known about Nature. We know that life exists on earth, we know a lot about how it manages to survive, and we are fairly confident that the nature of living things changes gradually through the process of evolution driven by natural selection. Any attempt to fill in the details of the history of the origin and evolution of life must be regarded with a certain suspicion, since it will deal with events of long ago to which nobody was witness. Nonetheless, biologists believe they can assemble a fairly accurate account of the major highlights of life's history. Let me now give you a very quick version, uncritically, leaving you to consult *The Creation of Life*, or other similar books if you prefer a more considered appraisal.

Most chemists and biologists believe that life began when aggregates of chemicals began to make more of themselves. The favoured candidates for these first 'reproducers' are simple nucleic acids similar to the DNA and RNA of modern life. They are supposed to have formed spontaneously from the 'primordial soup' of the planet, and had the ability to catalyse the chemistry needed for their own multiplication. Some people believe that the first chemicals able to make more of themselves may have borne no resemblance to modern nucleic acids; but most agree that eventually nucleic acids able to encourage their own replication did arise, even if they were not first on the scene.

At some point, variants of these first nucleic acids arose which were able to direct a form of protein manufacture; and then the first cells, presumably just membrane-bound aggregates of a few nucleic acids and proteins, would have formed, encouraged to do so by the chemicals within them. The raw materials needed to sustain these cells would have been taken up from the environment and used with very little processing, since the many enzymes of modern life were not available. All the chemical reactions sustaining the earliest cells must have been energetically favourable (that is, liable to proceed spontaneously) in their own right, or must have been coupled to other energetically favourable reactions in very simple ways. The cells would largely be sustained by reactions between high energy chemicals gathered from the environment, whose formation would have been powered by the energy of sunlight, or the heat of volcanic activity, natural radioactive decay, or perhaps the energy released by meteorites as they bombarded the planet's surface.

As evolution proceeded, the nucleic acids at the heart of cells would have grown longer and more complex, able to generate many more proteins with ever-increasing accuracy. The battery of proteins available would have been perfected, through the evolution of the genes that encoded them, into ever more efficient catalysts. They would have become able to process the raw materials of the environment in increasingly complex ways, allowing, for example, energy available within chemicals of the environment to be captured and stored in the form of various high energy chemicals made within the cell until the energy was required by the chemistry of the cell.

Eventually, some cells must have arisen whose proteins and membranes and metabolites allowed them to capture the energy of sunlight directly and use it to manufacture high energy chemicals such as carbohydrates and hence drive forward all of the energy-requiring reactions of the cell – photosynthesis would have begun.

One of the most significant developments in the evolution of life on earth must have been when some of the early simple cells began to live within other cells. Some of these gate-crashers would then have evolved into the internal organelles, such as mitochondria, chloroplasts, etc., of present-day life.

Another momentous phase began when cells started to interact with one another before giving rise to progeny, rather than each cell simply splitting in two. When cells came together before reproducing they became able to create offspring containing genetic information derived from both parents, thus beginning the process of sexual reproduction.

Some time after the origin of sex, and perhaps thanks to the increased possibilities for variation and evolution which sex made possible, cells began to live permanently attached to one another in the form of the first simple multicellular organisms. Cells, which had previously been aggressively independent individualists, discovered the advantages of communal life.

The fossil record reveals how rapidly multicellular life prospered and diversified. There began a process of increasing 'division of labour' between the different cells of multicellular life – some becoming specialized for gathering food for all the other cells, some becoming specialized to give the organism the ability to move, some becoming specialized for defence against other organisms, and so on . . .

Multicellular creatures soon began to develop distinct tissues and organs in which groups of related types of cells performed specialized tasks for the benefit of the organism as a whole. They began to develop a distinct 'body cavity' or 'coelom' in which many of the organs were found. They began to develop hard outer shells or internal skeletons and nerves and muscles which allowed them to swim through the water and then crawl onto the land. Locomotion was virtually exclusive to the animals, allowing them to rush about and eat one another and also eat plants. Plants survived, however, because they had learned the crucial trick of photosynthesis which ensured that animals could never survive without them.

It has taken several billion years for evolution driven by natural selection to create the creatures of the modern world; and the evolutionary process will continue to shape the populations of the future. It has so far furnished the world with an astonishing diversity of complex forms of life, and yet at heart it all depends on the simple ability of things to make other things which are very similar to themselves but usually slightly different.

But what *is* life?

In this chapter and the previous one, I have glibly used the term 'life' on the assumption that everyone knows and agrees what it really means. This is a fair assumption if all we require is some general comprehension of what is 'living' and what is 'dead'; but life is such an important part of Nature that its definition should perhaps be pinned down completely and unambiguously. The problem is that life cannot be defined unambiguously, at least not in a manner that satisfies everyone's intuitive impression of what life means. So I cannot answer the question posed at the head of this section, but it is worthwhile, briefly, to consider the problem.

Most non-scientists feel that there must be some clear-cut distinction between the living and the non-living world, because the difference between the things they most readily identify as living and others they readily identify as non-living is obvious. Few people would contend that a rock is alive, while everyone can agree that they themselves, their pet cat, and even a flea on their pet cat, are all most certainly alive. Such clarity, however, stems from examining Nature at its *extremes*. Just as a beach is obviously 'low ground' and a mountain top is obviously 'high ground', so a rock is obviously not alive and we obviously are alive. But as you

157

ascend from a beach towards a mountain top, where does the low ground end and the high ground begin? Most people are happy to accept this as a rather pointless, even silly, question. They have no trouble accepting that 'low ground' and 'high ground' are imprecise and relative terms with no clear point at which one gives way to the other. 'Life' appears to be a similarly imprecise term. The fact that many people have difficulty in accepting this suggests that they are reluctant to recognize their 'brotherhood' with rocks and mud and stones as fellow aggregates of the matter which makes up the universe.

All this does not imply that there is no strict definition which can be given to the term 'life'. There is a fairly good one, as you shall see; but unfortunately it confers the honourable title of 'living things' upon what most people would intuitively dismiss as 'mere chemicals'. All the creatures that everyone accepts to be alive without question are believed to have been derived from simpler creatures, or even just simpler 'things', by the process of evolution. The ability to evolve by natural selection is what allowed simple things to give rise to the very complex living things of today. So the one single simple definition of living things that makes any sense, is to say that living things are those things that have the ability to evolve by natural selection. That is not the only definition offered by modern science, but it is increasingly recognized to be the best one. Sadly, it means that a hot rock pool on the primordial earth, containing molecules of nucleic acid able to make more of themselves thanks to the process of complementary base-pairing, would be described as containing life. The natural, intuitive, response to that assertion is to shake one's head and decide that our definition of life must be wrong, for the rock pool clearly contains mere chemicals participating blindly in chemical reactions driven only by physical law. There's the rub: any definition of life seems to diminish its stature, and therefore our stature, down from noble free-thinking beings to 'mere' chemicals interacting and reacting. There are two solutions to the dilemma: either we must accept that we are simply the creations of chemical reactions; or else we must seek refuge in metaphysical mysteries hidden from our scrutiny. Take your choice, or choose to sit bewildered on the fence (as I do); but at least accept that 'life' is a vague and imprecise term of only limited utility.

One final thought on the question of 'What exactly is life?'. Consider the answer 'What does it matter?'. Things we choose to call living and those we choose to call not living, whether they are stars, rocks, plants, humans or something else, all clearly exist, and change, and interact. It is the interactions and the changes that really matter, rather than the ways we choose to describe and classify them, which can change as our knowledge of Nature develops.

15 Brains

Each one of us is a conscious mind. We are aware that we exist, we can summon up memories of the past, envisage hopes and fears for the future and think abstract thoughts; yet nobody knows what all this mental activity really is or how it is created. Whatever it is, it depends upon the brain. We can injure a foot, or a leg, or lose a lung or even be given a new heart, and it will have no direct impact on our mind; but injuries to the brain can directly change our thoughts, memories and the very nature of what we are. There seems no doubt that the mind, which is all that 'we' really are, is created by the brain, or at the very least depends on the brain in order to exist and function. Some people are happy to simplify things by abolishing the concept of mind and declaring that each of us is a conscious brain – a mass of integrated chemistry that is somehow aware of its own existence. Others feel sure that the mind is something higher, more special, than the brain – perhaps part of a mysterious 'spiritual' domain of the universe which science knows nothing about. Yet, whatever stance one takes, the same conclusion must always be reached: we know nothing substantial about the way in which the structure and activities of a brain allow it to be aware of its own existence and to think.

That does not mean, of course, that nothing is known about what goes on in the brain. An enormous amount is known about the cells of the brain, especially its nerve cells, and the events within them that accompany the workings of a mind. Yet what we know is the detail without the global view. We are like people who can see lots of lights flashing on and off on the console of a complex machine, and who can even probe within the machine to investigate the wiring and the flow of electrons through its circuitry, but who have no real idea of how all this activity allows the machine to perform its overall function.

With that warning, we shall take a quick look inside the machinery of the brain to examine the nerve cells that are believed to be its most vital components. The brain contains lots of nerve cells. It also contains many other types of cells, but these are believed to play supporting roles assisting the nerve cells that really matter. What nerve cells seem to do is make contact with one another and affect one another's activities by passing waves of chemical activity along and between themselves. The wave-like signals are known as 'nerve impulses', and the brain appears to be a machine devoted to the generation, integration and control of nerve impulses. Changing patterns of nerve impulses come and go within the structure of the brain, and as a result, somehow, consciousness arises from the patterns; and that consciousness sees, hears, smells, feels, thinks, remembers and plans for the future. That, at least, is the best guess of modern science about the link between nervous activity and the mind.

Nerve cells vary greatly in their shape and structure, but all have a main 'cell body', many spidery extensions of the cell body known as 'dendrites', and a long limb known as an 'axon' which then ramifies into other spidery extensions known as the 'terminal branches' of the axon (see figure 15.1). The

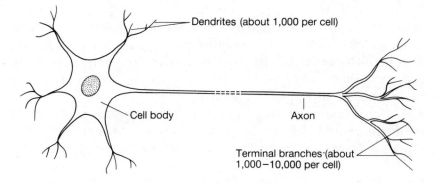

Figure 15.1 A nerve cell.

dendrites are the main parts of the cell that receive chemical signals from other cells, while the terminal branches are the parts that pass signals on to other cells. A nerve cell is a receiver, processor and transmitter of chemical signals.

The nerve signals are produced by the controlled and assisted movement of ions through the nerve cell membrane, causing changes in the distribution of electric charge between the inside and outside of the cell. The chemicals which control the movement of ions through the membrane are certain proteins; and we must consider five main types of protein to gain a general understanding of how nerve cells work.

One of these proteins is called the sodium/potassium pump, or simply the Na^+/K^+ pump, because it controls the flow of sodium ions (Na^+) and potassium ions (K^+) through the membrane. Molecules of this protein are found embedded in the nerve cell membrane, where they can bind to Na^+ ions inside the cell and transport them out, while also binding to K^+ ions outside of the cell and transporting them in. So, overall, the Na^+/K^+ pump pumps Na^+ions out of cells and pumps K^+ ions in (see figure 15.2a).

Another protein embedded in nerve cell membranes, known as the K^+ leak channel, allows some of the K^+ ions to leak out of the cell much more quickly than Na^+ ions are allowed to leak back in. So the net effect of the activity of both these proteins is to make the layer of solution just outside the cell membrane positively charged relative to the layer of cytosol just inside the cell; essentially because the K^+ leak channel lets K^+ ions leak to the outside without allowing an equivalent number of compensating Na^+ ions (or other positively charged ions) to leak back in. The membranes of all cells possess this charge imbalance, being slightly positively charged outside and relatively negatively charged inside, but nerve cell membranes make special use of it.

A nerve impulse begins when a chemical known as a neurotransmitter (of which there are many different types) is released from one nerve cell to bind to 'receptor' proteins

Figure 15.2 Summary of the most essential features of the creation and transmission of a nerve impulse.

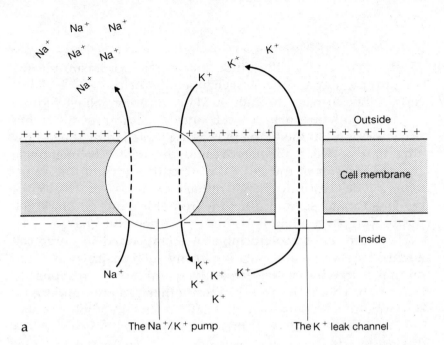

Outside

Cell membrane

Inside

a   The Na$^+$/K$^+$ pump   The K$^+$ leak channel

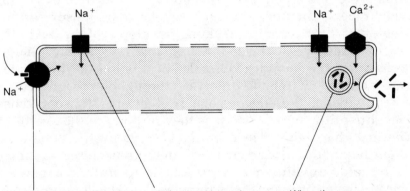

Neurotransmitter molecules bind to receptor proteins, causing these proteins to allow positive ions, such as Na$^+$, to flood into the cell and depolarize the membrane in the vicinity

Na$^+$ channel proteins are induced by the membrane depolarization to allow Na$^+$ ions to flow through them. This reverses the polarization of the membrane nearby. The polarization reversal in one region induces neighbouring Na$^+$ channels to open, causing a wave of polarization reversal to spread along the cell membrane

When the nerve impulse reaches the terminal branches it induces membrane proteins to allow Ca^{2+} ions to enter the cell. The Ca^{2+} ions induce vesicles containing neurotransmitter molecules to release these neurotransmitters, allowing them to bind to the next nerve cell

b

embedded in the membrane of another nerve cell (see figure 15.2b). As a result of the binding of the neurotransmitter, the receptor protein undergoes a change in structure which allows certain ions to pass through it. Many receptors allow sodium ions to flood into a nerve cell once a neurotransmitter has become bound to them, the ions being pulled in by the electric attraction between themselves and the relatively negatively charged interior of the cell. Of course, the entry of these ions tends to destroy the charge imbalance across the region of the membrane surrounding the receptor protein, since the positively charged Na^+ ions neutralize negative charge.

There are other protein molecules embedded in nerve cell membranes which are sensitive to any such destruction of the normal charge imbalance across the membrane. In response to the loss of charge imbalance these other proteins undergo a conformational change which briefly opens up a hole for Na^+ ions to pass through, and then quickly closes it again. While this protein is 'open' Na^+ ions flood in to such an extent that they reverse the normal charge imbalance of the surrounding region of the membrane, making the interior of the cell in that region positively charged rather than negatively charged relative to the outside. Molecules of this fourth vital protein are studded at regular intervals throughout the nerve cell membrane, so the effect of one of them opening soon causes neighbouring ones to open, as they respond to the loss of the normal charge imbalance brought about by the opening of their neighbour. So the effect of a neurotransmitter binding to a receptor protein in a nerve cell is to initiate a pulse of electrochemical change which travels quickly along the length of the nerve cell. The main effect of this change is for a wave of reversed charge imbalance (technically, 'polarization reversal') to spread along the membrane. This wave of reversed charge imbalance rushing along a nerve cell membrane is the electrochemical signal which we call a nerve impulse.

A nerve impulse really does spread as a discrete 'pulse' with regions of normal membrane charge imbalance both ahead of it and behind it, because as one region of the membrane is undergoing its reversal of charge imbalance, regions behind it (i.e. those which underwent their reversal earlier) are recovering their normal imbalance. This recovery occurs because, first, neurotransmitter molecules soon dissociate from their receptor proteins, returning the proteins to their normal 'closed' state; and second, because the other protein channels that open up to allow Na^+ ions to flood into the cell soon close and then return to their normal state, all of which allows the Na^+/K^+ pump and the K^+ leak channel to restore normality (often assisted by the activity of more proteins we need not consider here).

That, in briefest possible outline, is what a nerve impulse is and how it is created; but how does the passage of an impulse along one cell induce another cell 'connected' to this first cell to fire? When a nerve impulse arrives at a terminal branch of a nerve cell it encounters yet another type of protein embedded in the membrane. This protein is induced by the arrival of the impulse to allow calcium ions (Ca^{2+}) to enter the cell. These calcium ions alter the chemistry of tiny membrane-bound 'bags' (technically, 'vesicles'), found inside the end of nerve cells, which contain lots of neurotransmitter molecules. This alteration induces the membranes of the vesicles to fuse with the cell membrane in a way which allows the neurotransmitter molecules to be released into the space between connected nerve cells which is known as the 'synapse' between the cells. The neurotransmitters diffuse across this synapse, bind to the receptor proteins embedded in the membrane of the nerve cell on the other side of the synapse, and so induce a nerve impulse to travel along the next nerve cell. Thus the transmission of impulses along one nerve cell can induce the transmission of impulses along all the other cells to which that nerve cell is connected.

That covers the essence of nervous activity, but, as you might expect, there are lots of complications and complexities. Most individual nerve cells receive signals, in other words they receive neurotransmitters, from many other nerve cells; and they also pass on signals, via neurotransmitters, to many other nerve cells. There are lots of different types of neuro-transmitters, and while some of these encourage a nerve cell to 'fire' (that is, transmit an impulse) in the manner outlined above, others *inhibit* this firing. So in reality a nerve cell acts like a tiny chemical ballot machine. Its 'decision' to fire or not to fire, or to fire often or to fire rarely, depends on the result of a chemical 'election' in which the votes are the many and perhaps conflicting signals it receives from other cells. For most nerve cells, it is probably the *rate of firing* that is the true carrier of nervous information, rather than any individual impulse. Other complications, complexities and subtleties are far too numerous and intricate to be explored in a book such as this; but it is important to appreciate that they all involve 'mere' chemical effects, similar to the most vital ones outlined above, and all explicable in terms of the interactions and reactions between chemicals as they move about, collide with one another, and are pushed and pulled by the electric force and the tendency of energy to disperse towards a more even distribution.

So, even when we investigate the most complicated things we know of – our living brains – all we can find is chemistry underpinned by physics and integrated into the interacting networks of chemicals that we classify as biological systems. This does not mean that other, deeper secrets are not waiting to be discovered, or are perhaps forever going to remain hidden from our detection and understanding. As I have already said, science can certainly not provide a satisfactory explanation, or even description, of the origin of conscious minds from the physical, chemical and biological phenomena that we find within the brain. All that has been found in the brain is an incredibly complex network of interconnected nerve cells which pass nerve impulses along their lengths and pass a variety of chemical signals on to other nerve cells which encourage, inhibit, or otherwise modify the impulses which pass along these other nerve cells. The general assumption of the scientific establishment is that consciousness, with all its mental sensations and thoughts and ideas, is what happens (somehow!) within a brain when its network of nerves undergoes specific and no doubt very complicated patterns of firing. That assumption remains unproven, and may be wrong.

When we 'remember' something our brain is presumed to generate a pattern of nervous activity which in some crucial way resembles the pattern which was brought about by our initial experience of the thing we are remembering. Most theories of memory depend on molecular mechanisms that would allow the occurrence of a specific pattern of nervous activity to make it easier for the same pattern, or a similar one, to arise again. So something which has happened once in our brains would be more likely to happen again than something which has never happened; and we can somehow encourage the repeat performances of previous nervous activity to appear within our heads when we command them to.

Theories about the origin of mental activity and memory abound, and some of the books listed in the bibliography will help you explore these theories if you wish, but facts are rare. Nothing about the subtle details of our minds, our thoughts and our memories has been pinned down to the level of specific physical, chemical and biological processes.

One particular aspect of our minds which science cannot yet help us with concerns the free will that most of us believe we possess – the freedom to decide to do one thing or another, and to think one thing or another, without mere chemistry dictating to us what we will do. Perhaps the most significant question facing mankind is the one that asks whether our apparent free will is a reality or an illusion, but sadly it is a question which cannot yet be answered. While totalitarian determinism reigned over science the prospects for free will seemed bleak indeed, unless it involved some aphysical spiritual phenomena which were unfettered by deterministic physics. The rise of quantum mechanics and its uncertainty principle has offered hope to many believers in free will, supposedly leaving scope for the mind to choose specific eventualities out of the range of quantum mechanical probabilities in some mysterious way. Again, theories abound, but none yet looks at all convincing, and it would not be appropriate to dig into such speculations here. Physics, chemistry and biology may all eventually come together to offer us deep insights into how our brains generate our conscious minds, but they are far from doing so at present. In a review of our most basic knowledge of Nature it is fair to describe the mind as a hidden inner chamber of Nature whose secrets have yet to be revealed.

16 Mysteries

We are used to admiring the achievements of science, the deep understanding of, and ability to exploit, the natural world that the scientific method of enquiry and reason has brought. This book has offered a broad view of the foundations of Nature revealed by science, and the suggestions for further reading in the bibliography offer a route towards a closer, more detailed view of Nature and our predicament within it. Yet, as we admire the achievements of science, it is easy to lose sight of the many mysteries that remain; and one of the troubling things about these mysteries is that they often concern the questions we would most like answered. So, to round off 15 chapters in which I have trumpeted the triumphs of science I want to redress the balance with a very quick summary of just some of the major mysteries that remain. In doing so, I shall follow the pattern of the book as a whole, beginning with fundamental physics and cosmology and then moving upwards to consider the major mysteries currently facing biology.

Everything that happens in the universe, all physics, all chemistry, all biology, is powered by the 'winding down' process known technically as the increase in entropy, and colloquially as the spread of disorder due to the relentless dispersal of energy. This winding down process gives direction to 'the arrow of time' pointing us forever into the future and forbidding any return to the past, indeed it is what makes the future different from the past; but what originally 'wound the universe up'? Where did its initial ordered and concentrated energy (its initial low entropy) come from? This has been described as the central mystery of physics, and without an answer we cannot pretend to understand the universe which made us. Many possible answers have been suggested, but none yet looks fully convincing or has been described in an appropriately rigorous mathematical form.

We also do not know the ultimate fate of the universe. Will it expand forever into a cold dead eternal future, or collapse back into a 'big crunch' which might precede a new big bang and a new beginning? The crucial determinant of this fate would seem to be the total mass of the universe. If it exceeds a certain value then its mutual gravitational attraction will eventually pull everything inwards towards a big crunch. If there is insufficient mass then perpetual expansion into cold nothingness would seem to be our fate. The true value of the universe's mass is not yet known, but is eagerly being sought.

The real nature of empty space (or, strictly, spacetime) also remains a tantalizing mystery. We have seen that, to physicists, space is not nothingness, but a phenomenon with deep and subtle structure. How many dimensions are there to it? Is it a continuous entity or composed of a lattice of closely spaced discrete points? Are all particles and all forces merely the consequences of mysterious twists in spacetime? The answers to such questions are crucial to a full understanding of Nature, but they remain unknown.

In modern physics all of the things that seem to be particles and all of the things that seem to be waves in fact possess characteristics of both particles and waves, and their behaviour is described by the theory known as quantum mechanics. The mathematics of quantum mechanics, however, can never tell us with certainty what a physical system is doing or what it will do in the future. The conventional interpretation of the mathematical procedures of quantum mechanics is that they reveal only statistical, probabilistic, information about a world which seems to crystallize out of many possibilities each time we investigate it; but there are other, rival, interpretations, and great mysteries surrounding even the conventional view. Some physicists feel that quantum theory is incomplete, and that when it is complete its statistical probabilistic elements may be removed. So what is the correct interpretation of quantum mechanics, the theory that gives us our best description yet of the micro-world, and are there further developments needed to complete that description?

Another mystery, related to quantum mechanics, is that experiments in fundamental physics have revealed mysterious connections, or correlations, between particles that are far apart – so far that anything passing between them would need to move faster than light to be responsible for the effects observed. Physicists have good reason to reject faster than light signalling, so what do these experiments imply about the nature of the universe and the connections between its parts? What explanations can be offered for this mystery?

This book has sought out the simplicities that lie at the heart of all the complexity of the universe, but the details of the complexity remain there waiting to be solved. How, in detail rather than outline, do complex systems emerge from the interaction of simple parts? For centuries people have tried to glean understanding of natural processes by reducing them to their simplest parts operating in simple circumstances. Such an approach leaves unsolved many of the mysteries associated with complex systems. The emerging science of chaos is beginning to unravel something of the nature of complexity, but we are far from a true understanding of most of the complex phenomena around us and within us.

There are mysteries in chemistry, the central science, but none so fundamental as those facing physicists and biologists. Chemists would dearly like to know more about the precise mechanisms by which reactions proceed, the exact intricate steps followed by electrons and nuclei in what I have described as their 'frantic dance'. There are also two rather different theories or 'models' in use to describe the exact nature of chemical bonds, one known as the 'valence bond' approach and the other as the 'molecular orbital' approach. The contest between these two approaches does not affect the basic outline of chemical bonding given in this book, since that outline concentrated on central principles shared by both; but it is true to say that chemists still lack a single satisfactory mathematical description of the full details of chemical bonding.

Moving to biology, we meet the problem of how adult multicellular organisms such as humans arise from single cells. We know that this development process is determined by an interaction between the original cell's genes and its environment, but very little is known about exactly how a creature as complex as a human being emerges from the interaction. Even in the age of genetic engineering and test-tube babies, much of what happens in the womb remains a mystery.

When we search within the brains which we believe give rise to our minds, we can find nothing but living cells composed of chemicals. We know much about how these cells can pass electrochemical signals between themselves, but nothing about they way in which they create our conscious minds, assuming they do. To understand, or at least more properly *describe*, the origin of consciousness is surely the ultimate challenge facing us. It may well be an impossible challenge, but we should at least accept that science cannot currently tell us anything fundamental about how conscious minds arise, become aware, and then dissipate as time flows on.

Related to the puzzle of the mind, the phenomenon of memory is another enigma, albeit one that is likely to be understood more easily than the problem of consciousness. Simple creatures which we are reluctant to regard as conscious do display powerful and complex effects of memory. Research is beginning to uncover some of the mysteries of memory in such simple creatures, and the results may shed light on the still deep mystery of the nature and origin of our own memories.

Thinking about the mind also returns us to the fundamental problem of free will: the question of how the 'blind laws of physics' allow us to take decisions, or in other words possess 'free will' – or do they? The answer to this problem will, of course, be related to the answer to the mystery of consciousness, but there are two separate mysteries involved. In principle, consciousness might arise with either true free will available to it, or perhaps just the illusion of free will hiding a complex mix of chance and determinism. We do not know whether our own apparent free will is real or illusory, and it will be very difficult to find out.

171

Evolution is an area in which mystery can be expected, since while the most significant parts of the evolution of life were occurring there was nobody around intelligent enough to study it and bear reliable witness. Recent research on bacteria has revealed a puzzling ability to, seemingly, generate specific mutations in response to a specific need. This contradicts the established doctrine that the mutations that power evolution are random, or at least not directed towards any pre-existing need. A powerful and previously unrecognized mechanism of evolution may be awaiting detection.

Of course the first spark of evolution was the origin of life. Despite many years of research and speculation, the way in which life first arose remains a mystery. We do not know for sure whether the life we are descended from first arose on the earth or elsewhere. We do not know the chemical paths that presumably allowed a mixture of primordial chemicals to interact and react to create the first reproducing and evolving systems required to set life on its way. There are theories which are held so forcefully that elementary textbooks often present them as proven facts, but the theories change as fashions come and go, and all remain unproven and often supported by very little hard experimental evidence.

Nor do we know if we are alone in the universe, or if it is teeming with extraterrestrials living on a multitude of other worlds. Rational argument suggests that either we are alone, or we are just one member of a vast living horde. There are also lines of argument which suggest the likely nature of extra-terrestrial life; and the search for signs of such life has begun.

Turning to the things that go wrong with us as we deteriorate and die, the exact causes of many diseases remain at least partly mysterious – cancer, heart disease and various dementias to name just a few. Also, some very distressing and fatal diseases are caused by infectious agents whose actual nature remains mysterious. They have been called 'slow viruses', or 'prions' or 'virinos', yet nobody knows what they are or exactly how they work. They have been publicized (in Britain, at least) as the cause of Bovine Spongiform Encephalopathy (BSE) which is believed to be related to the similar sheep disease called scrapie, and to have been transmitted to cattle by the use of uncooked sheep meat and offal in cattle feed. The agents responsible for BSE, scrapie, the related 'Creutzfeld-Jakob syndrome' in humans and other similar diseases may represent an entirely new class of infectious agents which may be responsible for many of the slow degenerative diseases whose causes are currently unknown.

Finally, death is the one certainty in the future of each of us, but why do our bodies age and then die? Some biologists take the view that we are 'programmed to die' through the action of genes which have evolved through natural selection. Others feel that random chemical damage and the second law of thermodynamics are more to blame, causing crucial bits of us to simply 'wear out' and lose their place in the complex network of interactions that keeps us alive. Theories abound, backed up by some evidence, but it will be a long time before we fully understand this final phenomenon of life.

So we should let nobody convince us that science is 'nearly finished', or that 'almost everything that there is to be known is known', as some people try to do. If we stand back and survey the achievements of science alongside the mysteries that remain, it is perhaps easier to conclude that science has barely begun.

There is certainly a very full agenda of mystery to apply the scientific method to as we move into the twenty-first century. We have discovered much about Nature, and have many achievements to be proud of, but much, much more remains to be discovered and to be done . . .

Glossary

This is a summary of the main technical terms used in this book in the context in which they are used in the book. A few of the terms can be used in various other ways in different contexts. This glossary is provided merely as a simple aid to readers as they work through the book.

Activation energy   The energy needed to activate chemicals into participating in a particular chemical reaction.

Adenine   One of the bases found in DNA and RNA. It pairs with thymine in DNA and uracil in RNA to form A–T or A–U base-pairs.

Amino acids   The simple chemical building blocks of all proteins. Twenty different amino acids are available to make proteins, in which they are found linked up into long chains of specific 'amino acid sequences'.

Anticodon   A group of three bases on a transfer RNA molecule which can form base-pairs with a complementary codon on messenger RNA, and so allow the codon to specify the incorporation of a particular amino acid (carried by the transfer RNA) into a growing protein chain.

Atomic number   The number of protons in an atom.

Atoms   The basic particles of chemistry, composed of protons and neutrons in a central nucleus which is surrounded by electrons.

Axon The long extension of a nerve cell which conducts nerve impulses away from the nerve cell body and towards the cell's terminal branches.

Base-pair Two complementary bases of DNA or RNA held together by weak forces of attraction.

Bases (of DNA or RNA) Chemical components of the molecules known as 'nucleotides' which are linked together to form the nucleic acids DNA or RNA. Each base can form a base-pair with a specific complementary base on another strand of a nucleic acid.

Big bang The instant at which all the spacetime, matter and energy of the universe is supposed to have burst forth from some incredibly tiny point to expand and cool to generate the, still expanding and cooling, universe we see today.

Big crunch The possible reversal of the big bang, in which all spacetime, matter and energy may collapse back into one incredibly tiny point.

Bond A chemical linkage between two atoms or ions.

Bosons A class of particles with zero or whole number (i.e. 0, 1, etc. but never fractions) values of spin, which includes the so-called 'messenger' particles believed to mediate the fundamental forces.

Catalyst A substance which speeds up a chemical reaction while itself remaining unchanged, overall, in the process.

Cell The basic unit of life. A cell consists of a membrane-bound sac of watery fluid, containing all the chemicals which allow the cell to live and reproduce.

Cell membrane The fatty membrane which forms the boundary of all cells.

Chaos A term used to describe complex, unpredictable and apparently random systems. The modern science of chaos is revealing that such systems may be described by pleasingly simple mathematical procedures.

Charge   A term used for the mysterious phenomenon that makes objects carrying the charge generate and feel the effects of a fundamental force. For example, objects carrying electric charge (which can be positive or negative) generate and feel the effects of the electromagnetic force.

Chromosome   A structure in the nucleus of a cell, composed of a portion of the cell's DNA plus various proteins bound to the DNA. All the genes of a cell are distributed between its various chromosomes.

Codon   A group of three bases which codes for the incorporation of a specific amino acid into a growing protein chain, by forming base-pairs with a complementary anticodon of transfer RNA.

Coenzyme   A chemical which becomes bound to an enzyme and so helps the enzyme to achieve its act of chemical catalysis.

Compound   Any chemical which is composed of two or more types of atoms or ions chemically bonded together by covalent, polar covalent or ionic bonds.

Compound ions   Ions that contain more than one type of atom chemically bonded together within the structure of the ion.

Covalent bond   A chemical bond between two atoms which is formed when electrons become shared between the atoms involved. Equal sharing results in a pure covalent bond, unequal sharing in a polar covalent bond.

Cytosine   One of the bases found in DNA and RNA. It pairs with guanine to form the G–C base-pair.

Cytosol   The fluid inside a cell, excluding all the organelles and the fluids these organelles contain.

Dendrite   A thin extension from the body of a nerve cell, whose major role is to receive nervous inputs from other nerve cells.

DNA   Deoxyribonucleic acid – the nucleic acid which carries the genetic information of most forms of life.

Double-helix A structure formed when two complementary DNA molecules become wound around one another in the form of two intertwined helices or spirals. This is the structure of the DNA which forms the genes and chromosomes of life.

Electric charge The positive or negative charge which makes objects carrying the charge generate and feel the effects of the electromagnetic force.

Electromagnetic force One of the fundamental forces of Nature. It is responsible for the force of attraction between objects carrying electric charges of opposite signs, and the force of repulsion between objects carrying electric charges of the same sign; and it is also responsible for the phenomenon of magnetism. It is probably a distinct aspect of the more general electroweak force, whose effects also include the weak nuclear force.

Electromagnetic radiation A form of energy, including visible light, radio waves, infra-red rays and x-rays, which can be transmitted through space to influence the electromagnetic behaviour of objects it interacts with. It consists of oscillating electromagnetic fields propagating at the speed of light, regarded, in particle terms, as a stream of photons.

Electron A sub-atomic particle which carries negative electrical charge, found in orbitals surrounding the nuclei of atoms.

Electronegativity A measure of the ability of an atom to draw electrons towards it while participating in a chemical bond.

Electroweak force The unified fundamental force of Nature whose twin aspects are the electromagnetic force and the weak nuclear force. The unity is only apparent at energies higher than those encountered in the everyday world.

Elements Substances composed of only one type of atom.

Energy An abstract concept associated with natural systems and formally defined as their ability to do work. Doing work involves bringing about movement against a fundamental force, so energy can be thought of as the ability to bring about movement against a fundamental force.

Entropy A measure of the extent to which the available energy has become dispersed throughout any physical system. The second law of thermodynamics states that the entropy of natural systems always increases, indicating that in any natural change energy always becomes dispersed, overall, towards a more even distribution. Entropy is often loosely described as a measure of the 'disorder' within a system.

Enzyme A protein molecule which acts as a biological catalyst, catalysing a specific chemical reaction involved in the chemistry of life.

Equilibrium The state a reversible chemical reaction settles into when the rates of the forward and reverse reactions become equal. Chemical reaction still proceeds, but without altering the total amounts of reactants or products present.

Evolution The process by which the earliest living things are believed to have given rise to all later forms of living things, and by which current life will generate the life-forms of the future. Evolution is believed to be caused by the natural selection of beneficial novelties generated in the genetic material of organisms by random, or at least undirected, mutations.

Expression of genes The complete decoding of the genetic information of a gene into a functional protein molecule, involving both the transcription of the gene into RNA and then the translation of the genetic information into the structure of a completed protein.

Field A physical quantity, such as the value and direction of the electromagnetic force, which varies from place to place within spacetime.

First law of thermodynamics The law of conservation of mass-energy, which states that the total amount of mass-energy in the universe is constant. Energy can be converted into the form of mass, and mass can be converted into energy, but the total amount of mass-energy is constant.

Force A pushing or pulling or changing effect brought about by one or more of the fundamental forces of Nature. A force is best regarded as an *interaction* between two or more objects, with the objects being influenced to an equal extent by their shared interaction.

Fundamental forces The four basic forces that are responsible for all of the pushing, pulling and changing required to make every event in the universe proceed, namely: the gravitational force, the electromagnetic force, the strong nuclear force and the weak nuclear force. The electromagnetic and weak nuclear forces are probably distinct aspects of the one unified electroweak force; and further unification of the forces may be revealed by future progress in fundamental physics.

Gene A region of DNA which encodes one protein molecule, or one functional RNA.

General theory of relativity The part of Albert Einstein's relativity theory that describes the physics of systems undergoing acceleration relative to one another, and which indicates the equivalence between acceleration and gravity which leads to the notion that the gravitational force is the result of the curvature of spacetime.

Genetic code The code that determines which codons on messenger RNA bring about the incorporation of which amino acids into a protein.

Gluons The particles that are believed to mediate the strong nuclear force.

Gravitational force One of the fundamental forces of Nature. It is responsible for the force of attraction between all objects with mass.

Gravitons The particles that are believed to mediate the gravitational force.

Ground state The state of an atom in which all of its electrons are in the lowest energy orbitals available.

Guanine One of the bases found in DNA and RNA. It pairs with cytosine to form the G–C base-pair.

179

Heat A quantitative measure of the kinetic energy of motion possessed by the particles of a substance.

Higher organism Organism whose cells contain a distinct nucleus, as opposed to lower organisms such as bacterial cells.

Hydrogen bond A weak chemical bond resulting from the electromagnetic attraction between a hydrogen atom carrying a slight positive charge (because it is at one end of a polar covalent bond) and another atom carrying a slight negative charge (because it is at one end of another polar covalent bond). Hydrogen bonds hold together the base-pairs of complementary nucleic acids. They also form between water molecules.

Inertia The tendency of an object with mass to preserve its state of motion or of rest. In other words, its tendency not to accelerate, decelerate or change direction, unless acted on by a force.

Interaction Another word for a force, and the preferred term amongst physicists for a force.

Interference The tendency of two or more waves to combine together to yield an 'interference pattern'.

Interference pattern The complicated waveform produced when two or more waves interfere with one another.

Ionic bond The force of electromagnetic attraction holding positively and negatively charged ions together.

Ions Electrically charged particles formed when atoms or molecules lose or gain electrons.

Isotopes Different atoms of the same element which differ in the number of neutrons they contain.

Kinetic energy The energy of motion associated with all moving objects.

Leptons The generic name of a class of fundamental particles, including the electron and electron-neutrino. They feel the electromagnetic and weak nuclear forces but not the strong nuclear force.

Light Electromagnetic radiation with a frequency lying within the range visible to humans. Sometimes used more loosely to refer to electromagnetic radiation in general.

Lower organism Organism whose cells do not contain a distinct nucleus, such as a bacterial cell.

Mass A quantitative measure of the force needed to change an object's motion by a given amount.

Mass number The total number of protons plus neutrons in an atom.

Matter The stuff from which everything with mass is made. Nowadays regarded as a form of energy which has mass and occupies some definite volume.

Messenger RNA (mRNA) The RNA copy of a gene which becomes bound to a ribosome and directs the manufacture of a specific protein.

Metabolism All of the chemical activities occurring within a living cell or organism.

Metabolites Chemicals that participate in metabolism.

Metallic bonds The chemical forces that hold the atoms of a metal together. They are believed to involve a mobile 'sea' of outer electrons being attracted to the positively charged ions within that sea.

Molecular orbital An electron orbital surrounding all of the atomic nuclei within a molecule.

Molecule A chemical particle composed of two or more atoms which are held together by covalent or polar covalent bonds.

Momentum The product of the mass and the velocity of an object.

Mutation In its most general usage, a mutation is any change imposed upon the genetic material, normally DNA, of an organism.

Natural selection The natural survival and proliferation of genes and organisms carrying mutations which help the affected genes and organisms to survive and proliferate. Believed to be the fundamental process responsible for directing the course of evolution.

Nerve impulse A pulse of electrochemical change which spreads across the membrane of a nerve cell.

Neurotransmitter A chemical released from a nerve cell and which can then bind to neighbouring nerve cells and either encourage them to fire or discourage them from firing, and perhaps also modulate their activities in other ways.

Neutron A sub-atomic particle which carries no net electrical charge. Found in the nucleus of atoms.

Nucleic acids Chemicals which form the genetic material of life – DNA and RNA. All nucleic acids are composed of chemicals called nucleotides linked up into long chains. Each nucleotide is itself composed of sugar and phosphate groups, which form the 'backbone' of the nucleic acid chain, and bases which are attached to that backbone.

Nucleus (of atom) The cluster of protons and neutrons found at the centre of an atom.

Nucleus (of cell) The organelle within a living cell which contains the cell's chromosomes.

Orbital A specific volume of space within an atom in which electrons (two at most) can be found.

Organelles Distinct organized structures within living cells, often bounded by their own membrane.

Particles Small bits of matter such as molecules, atoms, ions, electrons, protons, neutrons, quarks, etc.

Periodic table Table of the elements which is divided into horizontal 'periods' and vertical 'groups' (see figure 9.1).

Photons The quantum particles of electromagnetic fields.

Photosynthesis The process within plants in which light energy serves to initiate the chemical reactions that convert carbon dioxide and water into carbohydrates and oxygen gas.

Planck's constant A fundamental numerical constant of Nature which corresponds to a certain amount of 'action' (energy × time).

Polar covalent bond A chemical bond between two atoms which is formed when electrons become shared between the atoms, but shared unequally, so that one atom possesses a slight positive charge (δ^+) while the other possesses a slight negative charge (δ^-).

Potential energy A form of energy which things possess because their position involves some defiance of a fundamental force.

Proteins Giant molecules formed when many individual amino acids become linked together. They catalyse and control the chemical processes of life, as well as performing various structural and other roles.

Proton A sub-atomic particle which carries positive electrical charge. Found in the nucleus of atoms.

Quantum fluctuation A temporary quantum mechanical phenomenon, such as a virtual particle, which can exist because of the freedom allowed by the uncertainty principle.

Quantum mechanics Theory of mechanics that incorporates the quantization of energy, wave-particle duality and the uncertainty principle. The best theory available to explain the activities of the micro-world.

Quarks The generic name for a class of fundamental particles. They are the building blocks of protons and neutrons.

Relativistic mass The mass of an object once the effect of its motion relative to the person measuring the mass is taken into account. The relativistic mass is the rest mass of the object plus an additional amount of mass whose value depends on the velocity of the motion.

Relativity Physical theory developed by Albert Einstein which is normally regarded as two distinct theories: the theory of special relativity and the theory of general relativity.

Replication of DNA The copying of one DNA double-helix into two copies of itself.

Rest mass The mass of an object when it is at rest relative to the person measuring the mass.

Ribosomal RNA (rRNA) The RNA that is found as an integral part of a ribosome.

Ribosome The complex of proteins and RNAs on which protein synthesis takes place.

RNA Ribonucleic acid. The nucleic acid which acts as the intermediary between DNA and protein in the central chemical mechanism of life.

Second law of thermodynamics The law which states that in any natural process the entropy of the universe must increase overall.

Spacetime The 'arena' in which all events in the universe occur. It consists of the dimensions of space (certainly three but perhaps more) united in a rigorous mathematical manner with the one dimension of time.

Special theory of relativity The part of Albert Einstein's relativity theory that describes the effects found by observers moving relative to one another without any acceleration. It revealed the unity of space and time as spacetime, the interchangeability of mass and energy, and the phenomena of the contraction of space and the dilation of time for objects moving without acceleration relative to us.

Speed A quantitative measure of the distance travelled by a moving object in a given time.

Spin A subtle property of particles when described using the theory of quantum mechanics, formally defined as a particle's intrinsic angular momentum. It can be thought of loosely as a measure of the way in which the particle is spinning on its axis, although this is really just a rather inaccurate analogy which attempts to relate a fundamental quantum mechanical property to the sorts of properties we find objects possess in the everyday world.

Strong nuclear force One of the fundamental forces of Nature. It is responsible for holding protons and neutrons together in the nucleus of an atom, and for holding quarks together within protons and neutrons.

Synapse The space between two nerve cells, across which neurotransmitters diffuse to allow the activity of one nerve cell to influence the activity of another.

Thymine One of the bases found in DNA. It pairs with adenine to form the A–T base-pair.

Transcription The copying of a strand of DNA into a complementary strand of RNA.

Transfer RNAs (tRNAs) The RNA molecules that bring specific amino acids to the ribosome during protein synthesis and transfer them into a growing protein chain.

Translation The decoding of the genetic information (base sequence) of a messenger RNA into the amino acid sequence of the protein molecule which the messenger RNA encodes.

Uncertainty principle The central principle of quantum mechanics which states that the position and momentum of a particle do not have definite values at the same time. It can also be stated in terms of the uncertainty about the energy of a phenomenon and the time it lasts for.

Uracil One of the bases found in RNA. It pairs with adenine to form the A–U base-pair.

Van der Waals bonds Weak forces of attraction between chemicals caused by transient fluctuating partial charges on their surface created by the random motion of their electrons.

Velocity A quantitative measure of the speed with which an object is moving in a given direction.

Virtual particle   A particle which owes its temporary existence to the uncertainty principle of quantum mechanics, the most important examples of which are the messenger particles that mediate the fundamental forces.

W particles   One of the types of messenger particles which mediate the weak nuclear force.

Wave equation   The equation which allows all phenomena, whether normally regarded as particles or waves, to be described quantitatively as wave-like phenomena.

Wave-packet   A particle-like combination of waves in which most of the wave phenomena are localized within a small volume of space.

Weak nuclear force   One of the fundamental forces of Nature. It is responsible for some forms of radioactive decay within atomic nuclei. It is probably just one of the twin aspects of the electroweak force.

Weight   A quantitative measure of the force of attraction between the earth and the object whose weight is being determined.

Work   A quantitative measure of the energy transferred to an object when its state of rest or motion is changed by the action of a force. Work is done when an object is moved against the effect of a fundamental force.

Z particles   One of the types of messenger particles which mediate the weak nuclear force.

Bibliography

Here is a list of some readable books in which you will find further details of the subjects introduced in this book.

Physics

Peter W. Atkins, *The Second Law*, W. H. Freeman, 1984.
Paul Davies (ed.), *The New Physics*, Cambridge University Press, 1989.
Albert Einstein, *Relativity – The Special and the General Theory*, Methuen & Co., 1920.
James Gleick, *Chaos*, Heinemann, 1987.
Heinz R. Pagels, *The Cosmic Code*, Penguin Books, 1982.
B. K. Ridley, *Time, Space and Things*, Cambridge University Press, 1984.
Joseph Schwartz and Michael McGuinness, *Einstein for Beginners*, Writers and Readers Publishing Cooperative Society, 1979.
Julian Schwinger, *Einstein's Legacy*, Scientific American Books, 1986.
Euan Squires, *To Acknowledge the Wonder – The Story of Fundamental Physics*, Adam Hilger, 1985.
Ian Stewart, *Does God Play Dice?*, Basil Blackwell, 1989.

Chemistry

Peter W. Atkins, *Molecules*, W. H. Freeman, 1987.
John C. Kotz and Keith F. Purcell, *Chemistry and Chemical Reactivity*, Saunders College Publishing, 1987.

Bibliography

W. Graham Richards, *The Problems of Chemistry*, Oxford University Press, 1986.

Hazel Rossotti, *Introducing Chemistry*, Penguin, 1975.

Lionel Salem, *The Marvels of the Molecule*, VCH (W. Germany), 1987.

Andrew Scott, *Molecular Machinery – The Principles and Powers of Chemistry*, Basil Blackwell, 1989.

Biology

Colin Blakemore and Susan Greenfield (eds), *Mindwaves*, Basil Blackwell, 1987.

Richard Dawkins, *The Blind Watchmaker*, Penguin, 1988.

Richard Dawkins, *The Selfish Gene*, Oxford University Press, 1989.

Christian de Duve, *A Guided Tour of the Living Cell*, Scientific American Books, 1984.

Richard L. Gregory (ed.), *The Oxford Companion to the Mind*, Oxford University Press, 1987.

Stephen Rose, *The Chemistry of Life*, Penguin, 1979.

John Maynard Smith, *The Theory of Evolution*, Penguin, 1975.

Andrew Scott, *The Creation of Life*, Basil Blackwell, 1986.

Andrew Scott, *Vital Principles – The Molecular Mechanisms of Life*, Basil Blackwell, 1988.

Index